ACTA UNIVERSITATIS UPSALIENSIS
Studia Psychologica Upsaliensia
12

INSTRUCTION AND THE DEVELOPMENT OF MORAL JUDGMENT

by

Iordanis Kavathatzopoulos

UPPSALA 1988

Doctoral Dissertation at Uppsala University 1988

ISBN 91-554-2244-6
ISSN 0586-8858

ABSTRACT

Kavathatzopoulos, I., 1988. Instruction and the development of moral judgment. Acta Univ. Ups. *Studia Psychologica Upsaliensia* 12, 112 pp. Uppsala. ISBN 91-554-2244-6

In discussing the theories of moral development it is argued that there is an essential difference between Kohlberg and Piaget. Kohlberg studied the characteristics of the concrete-abstract dimension of the development of moral thinking towards the discovery of moral principles. Piaget, on the other hand, focused his interest on the formation of the autonomous moral function. He studied the process of development towards independent moral thinking and action as an adaptive process to social reality. However, he did not incorporate the role of instruction into his theory, regarding its positive impact on the acceleration of development.

Based on Vygotsky's critique of Piaget, and on certain aspects of the Piagetian theory itself, it is argued that it is possible to stimulate the acceleration of the development of moral thinking through suitable instructions. Indeed, two empirical studies of the concepts of Intention and Equality showed that simple instructions produced a quick, high, generalizable and stable shift to the higher phase of moral judgment. It was also shown that there was no difference in sex, and the age difference, obtained only in the first study, was not greater than three months. The same high effect of instruction was obtained in the second study, which also showed that the personal authority of the instructor/tester did not influence the effect of the instruction.

These results show that it might be possible, too, to accelerate the development towards Piagetian moral autonomy by using suitable instruction, but this can be studied only in a social situation where both thinking and action are involved.

Iordanis Kavathatzopoulos, Department of Psychology, Uppsala University, Box 227, S-751 04 Uppsala, Sweden.

Printed in Sweden by
Textgruppen i Uppsala AB, 1988

ACKNOWLEDGMENTS

I wish to thank my supervisor, Berndt Brehmer, for valuable advice and constant support during this study. I am also grateful to Ismini Yannopoulou-Mitsakou for her generous assistance and materials which she made available for my study. Mats Björkman, Alf Gabrielsson, Peter Thunberg, Kurt Bergling, Gunnar Goude, Bosse Johansson, Olga Panopoulou-Maratou and Ioannis Kugiumutzakis have given helpful suggestions and comments on my work. I wish also to express my gratitude to Georgios Rigas, Akrivi Konidari, Marie Clark Nelson, Michalis Kolonias, Kritos Raptis, Kostas Koukoulis, Inga Cederberg, Elsa Sjöberg, the Hellenic Ministry of Education, the Hellenic Institute in Stockholm, the Municipality of Stockholm, and the schools, the teachers and the children, who helped to make this study possible.

To act absolutely from virtue is nothing else in us than to act, to live, to preserve our being (three things which are essentially one) according to the guidance of reason, on the basis of each seeking his own good.

Benedict Spinoza, *Ethics*, Part IV, Prop. XXIV.

CONTENTS

PART ONE
THE THEORIES OF MORAL DEVELOPMENT

INTRODUCTION

Undoubtedly, morality plays a very significant role in human society. Good morality has always been considered necessary for society to function well. Consequently, the construction of good moral systems has occupied philosophy since antiquity, and it probably concerned man even earlier. Morality's value is inestimable, too, for the reproduction of the prevalent social system. Therefore it has been the great interest of the ruling classes through the ages to produce the moral system they thought served their interests in the best way, and to impose it on people's social thinking and action. Morality is often used as a weapon in social conflicts, not only between social classes, but between other groups or individuals as well. Many of these conflicts have been resolved through the imposition of the morality of the winner on the defeated.

The most salient feature of morality is that it guides social action through the individual's own mind and not as a result of the force of social authorities. Right and wrong, good and evil, although often not produced by the individuals themselves, and, although usually contradictory to their interests, are accepted by them and used in their social conduct. Of course, the individual or the social group does not accept automatically every "arbitrary" moral code that is presented to them. The acceptance of that morality must be dependent, to some degree, on its functionality, i.e., the morality has to provide some answers to the social problems of a society and improve in some way the individual's life in that society.

Morality then is social knowledge, i.e., knowledge about social relations and ways of action within these relations, although the empirical studies presented in this work are limited to the investigation of moral thinking. This knowledge is not different in principle from knowledge about physical relations and action. These are of the same nature and have the same function. Of course, there is a difference between them in content. The latter refers to physical reality and relations and the former to social reality and relations. On the other hand there is no difference with regard to the psychical functions and cognitive processes behind knowledge about both physical and social reality. When the individual faces the problem of perceiving, judging, thinking, and acting upon the social and physical world, he uses the same cognitive processes.

In contrast to physical knowledge, morality is often knowledge that does not evolve through scientific or logical methods. That is so, as sometimes in the case of physical knowledge as well, because its truth is dependent upon the level of functionality that is provided by it as a solution to the problems that are met by the individual as a moral subject. Despite the similar psychological function of social and physical knowledge, the former was never supposed to have the potential of being produced by scientific methods by the individual, the social group or the whole society, as is supposed to be possible for the latter.

Nevertheless, morality is an area that may be an object for psychological research. Still, we have to clarify the different meanings of the concept of morality. Many problems could arise in the coming analysis if these concepts are confused, something that is very difficult to avoid in this area of research.

First, it is a philosophical endeavour to define good and evil, to find out what is fair and just, what people ought to do and how they can reach the Good. It is clear that this is not of interest for a psychological study, and it would be wrong if such issues interfered here.

Secondly, there are psychological studies of morality which are usually concerned with the description of the prevalent characteristics of moral functioning. The most influential theory in this area is Kohlberg's stage theory. This theory attempts to describe the features of moral thought as a six stage developmental scale, and it does not consider the formation of independent scientific moral thought. Kohlberg is not primarily interested in the process of production or acceptance of moral principles by the individual; rather he takes them for granted.

The third way to study morality is the Piagetian method. Piaget's main interest was in the development of the child's knowledge functions in relation to the physical world. He has also offered a theory of the development of autonomous moral thinking and action, and he was first to understand it as a necessary condition for the production of adaptive social knowledge. He studied the process towards independence and higher thinking: from a condition of authority constraint to the phase of independent scientific production of moral rules and principles, i.e., the heteronomy-autonomy dimension. The idea central to Piaget's theory is the individual's effort to adapt to physical and social reality. This is possible through actions guided by higher formal thinking which in turn is a result of the adaptive process. According to Piaget, this is also an independence and liberation process from any kind of physical as well as social constraint. On the other hand, Piaget did not incorporate into his theory the positive impact that social influence may have on the development towards independent moral functioning. Vygotsky criticized Piaget on this point and showed that it is possible to aid the development of logico-mathematical thinking through instruction. That critique was based on a different theoretical understanding of the role of language and of the relationship of the child to the social world around him. Indeed, Piaget accepted Vygotsky's critique, so that we may regard these two theories as one. They are complementary to one another.

The subject of the present thesis is to discuss the contributions of psychology to the area of moral development from a Piagetian-Vygotskian perspective, and to study its implications in an initial empirical investigation.

The first part of the discussion concerns Kohlberg's theory. That is necessary since that theory is the most influential one and has dominated the area of moral development for more than twenty years. Furthermore, Kohlberg's assertion that his theory is based on Piaget and, especially, some attempts made in the past to explain some observed effects of instruction on the acceleration of the Piagetian moral development by using Kohlberg's theory make it necessary to clarify the relationship between Kohlberg and Piaget.

Some theoretical implications for the thought-action problem are also important. While this is a problem for Kohlberg, since his theory investigates only moral thinking, Piaget (1932) has shown that these two can be studied together. Moreover, Piaget's theory does not isolate the one from the other but understands development as an interplay between thought and action. On the other hand, that does not mean that the investigation of the development of some Piagetian moral concepts, as in the present studies, is sufficient to make inferences about moral action as well.

The emotional aspect of moral thought and action is not considered in the present thesis. Although it is broadly accepted that emotions are strongly connected with the development of moral thinking, and more often with the development of moral action, advancement towards independent moral thinking and action has very little to do with emotions. Rather, such development is contradictory to emotions since they can impede the autonomous moral function. Emotions imply a confusion of perception, judgment and action in the same process. It is an automatic production of knowledge and action which does not allow a critical consideration of the whole social situation, i.e., a broad and deep consideration of the interests of the individual or of his social group, the existing social relations, the possibility to cooperate, etc., necessary for the formation of suitable moral principles and rules leading to corresponding action. Nevertheless, emotions may be important for the development of independent moral thinking. The feeling of happiness to adapt to the ever changing social world is very important, such as the feeling of responsibility for the individual himself and for his social group or the whole society, when he is at the autonomous phase. Still, these feelings and emotions are considered to be "outside" the function of the moral thinking process itself.

Rather, these are understood as providing considerable aid to the initiation and the maintenance of the autonomous moral process. That means that the formation of autonomous moral thinking is not understood, in the present work, as an ego-strengthening process, but rather as a pure cognitive process.

THE STAGE THEORY OF MORAL DEVELOPMENT

The structure of Kohlberg's theory

Lawrence Kohlberg is undoubtedly the most influential theorist in the area of moral development. His doctoral dissertation in 1958 was the beginning of a long tradition. His theory inspired many researchers and resulted in voluminous scientific reports, articles and books.

The theory that Kohlberg proposed in 1958 and developed later, is partially influenced by Piaget's theory. But Piaget's (1932) two phase theory was transformed into a six stage theory. Kohlberg (1969) described his theory as a cognitive-developmental theory. That means that:

1. the development of moral thinking involves transformations of cognitive structures and this development can only be described as a system of organizational wholes, i.e., stages,
2. this development is not the direct result of maturation or the direct result of learning, but it is caused by the interaction of the individual's cognitive structure with the structure of the environment,
3. the cognitive structures are structures of action,
4. development is directed towards a greater equilibrium between the aforementioned interaction, i.e., an equilibrium between the actions of the self and those of others towards the self,
5. there is no difference in principle between the processes of development of moral thinking to the processes of development of "physical" thinking, except that the former involves role-taking,
6. and there is a unity of the level of social and moral development due to cognitive development and due to ego development (Loevinger, 1966, 1976).

This cognitive-developmental approach implies, in short, that thought is developed through the interaction between the individual and the outside world, which leads to distinct cognitive structures as a result of the obtained equilibrium. These cognitive structures are stages of thought.

The hypothesis of *qualitatively different stages* is, according to Kohlberg, the core of the cognitive-developmental position, and he, by referring to

Piaget, considers that the cognitive stages must have the following characteristics:

1. Stages form an *invariant sequence*. The individual follows the same order of stages. He never skips a stage and proceeds always to the higher-order stage. This sequence may be slowed down or speeded up depending on cultural factors, but its order can not be changed.
2. Stages are *hierarchical integrations*. Moving to a higher mode of thinking results in a displacement of the lower stages. These do not disappear but continue to be used under the influence of and the preference for the new higher stage.
3. Stages are *structured wholes*. The thinking at a certain stage is always consistent with that stage. It represents the underlying cognitive structure organization of that stage.

The most salient characteristic of the Kohlbergian theory is the description of moral development as a sequence of three levels and six stages. The development is understood as a movement to higher, more abstract and inclusive moral principles which regulate the moral thinking of the individual.

The next step should be to present each stage and level. But there is some difficulty, since a lot of different versions are given by Kohlberg himself and by his associates (Kohlberg, 1963, 1966, 1976, 1981; Rest, Turiel & Kohlberg, 1969; Turiel, 1974; Turiel & Rothman, 1972; Haan, Smith & Block, 1968). Bergling (1981) has given a table with these different versions, but we are going to consider only the latest version by Kohlberg himself (Kohlberg, 1981, p. 409). One more reason to do this is the acceptance of a transitional stage, a phenomenon that Turiel (1974) observed in studying the equilibration process.

There are three levels of morality, each of which consists of two stages. The difference between these levels is based on the moral principles to which the individual directs himself. The preconventional moral level refers to children, as well as to some adults who have not yet come to understand and uphold conventional rules and expectations. On the conventional level most adolescents and adults accept the societal rules and conventions such as they are. On the postconventional level, which is reached by a minority of adults, the individual not only accepts the society's rules, but he is able to address his moral thinking to more general and higher moral principles that underlie these rules. But to come up on this level of moral thinking, it is necessary to acquire first the ability of formal operations.

The six moral stages, which are grouped two by two in these levels, have a hierarchical relationship to each other between the levels and inside the levels. The first of the two stages is always an entrance to each level, while the second stage expresses better the content of the level to which it belongs. Recently, Kohlberg (Kohlberg & Candee, 1984a) hypothesized the existence of two types of substages (type A and type B) as a solution to the thought-action problem.

As we have seen, stage sequence is invariant and stages are hierarchically related. That means, that the individual not only transforms the previous stage into a new structure, but that he prefers to reason in the highest stage he is capable of understanding (Rest, 1973). These six stages point to a movement, a development from the lower stages in the hierarchy to the higher.

The "how" is answered by reference to Piaget's equilibration process, and it has been studied by Turiel. However, the "why", the philosophical question behind Kohlberg's theory of moral development, is answered by reference to Plato (Kohlberg, 1981). The movement towards higher stages is explained by the platonic notion of the individual tending to narrow an ideal form of moral principle. In this case the ideal form of "Justice":

> . . . the individual intuitively appreciates a developmental hierarchy and will prefer a higher-level statement over a lower-level regardless of his own place in hierarchy, as long as he is capable of recognizing the difference between one level and the next.
> (Rest, Turiel & Kohlberg, 1969, p. 242)

Obviously, the development of moral thinking (in a Kohlbergian sense) is dependent upon intellectual processes inside the individual and not in confrontation with the outside world. That has some implications for the method which Kohlberg uses to study moral development.

Kohlberg is approaching the process of moral development through the creation of some kind of cognitive conflict (dilemma) in the subject's mind, by telling him a hypothetical story. The subject then gives a solution to the problem. He chooses one position and motivates his answer. These are the data on which the placement of the subject in the stage-hierarchy is based. The story most often referred to is the Heinz dilemma (Kohlberg, 1981, p. 12).

After telling the story, the experimenter asks several questions which prompt the subject to motivate his solution of the dilemma. Different stories and the following questions refer to different aspects of moral thinking. In the case of the "Heinz dilemma," the aspect of the value of human life and the aspect of the obligation to follow the law are contrasted. Other stories actualize other aspects such as the need for justice, promise breaking, the value of property, and punishment. The purpose of the interview that follows is to describe the structure and the content of the answers. It is very important to note that the definition of the subject's stage is always obtained through the interviews on several dilemmas. Some answers typical to "Heinz dilemma" are presented by Kohlberg (1985, pp. 29—31).

In the first studies, Kohlberg and his associates, presented nine stories in a clinical interview setting. That oral method caused some difficulties with the coding of data. Later, they developed three forms of dilemmas, A, B, and C (Colby et al., 1983), about the same moral aspects, and they asked the subjects to give written answers. This method may produce more easily coded material, but the interviewer loses much information. There are some problems, too, about the consistency of such a method with a constructivist theory (Weinreich-Haste, 1983). Rest (1979) has attempted to overcome those problems by constructing the Defining Issues Test (DIT), which is a multiple-choice questionnaire. The individual has the chance to choose higher moral judgments, and he usually does it more than in Kohlberg's original tests. This is a serious problem for DIT, as a descriptive test, although it was known from the studies of Rest et al. (1969) and Turiel (1966) that individuals prefer higher stage thought to their present stage.

Support for Kohlberg's theory

There is a considerable amount of research which supports the stage hypothesis. Those studies have tested the different characteristics of the process of moral development.

Kohlberg (1963) found that the percentage of higher-stage judgments increased with age and that lower-stage judgments decreased. That study supported the sequentiality hypothesis. It is important to mention that a number of 6th type judgments was obtained in that study, but that was not possible in Kohlberg's later studies (Colby et al., 1983).

Similar results were obtained in a study of the development of concepts of law and legal justice (Tapp & Kohlberg, 1971), of moral judgment in adolescent males (Page, 1981), and of role-playing induction of thinking one or two stages above (Walker, 1982).

Rest, Turiel and Kohlberg (1969) found also that the induction of advice from one stage higher, after the presentation of the moral dilemma, causes change towards the the next higher-stage thinking, while the presentation of lower-stage thinking does not cause regression to that lower stage.

The hierarchical nature of stages was studied by Rest (1973). He found that, as subjects comprehended various stages of moral thinking, they tended to prefer the highest stage comprehended. It was shown that comprehension of the statements ordered by stage was increasingly difficult. Turiel (1966, 1969, 1974, 1977; Turiel & Rothman, 1972), too, in studying the equilibration process as the underlying mechanism, was able to show the sequentiality, hierarchy, and distinctiveness of the stages.

Another characteristic of that theory is its universality hypothesis. The development of moral thinking through the six stage sequence is supposed to hold for people in different cultures as well as for both sexes. Indeed, Kohlberg and Kramer (1969) found that the stages of moral development form a universal invariant sequence in USA, Mexico, Taiwan, Turkey, and Yucatan. The sequence is not affected by culture. It is only the rate of the sequence that is affected. Middle-class urban individuals were found to be more advanced in moral judgment, than individuals who lived in isolated villages in Turkey and Yucatan. Studies in other countries, such as Moir (1974) in New Zealand, Parikh (1980) in India, and Nisan and Kohlberg (1982) in Turkey, provided further support for the universality claim.

Another area of research has been the relationship between logical and moral thinking. It is assumed that a stage of cognitive development is a prerequisite for the occurrence of moral thinking at a certain stage. Indeed, Tomlinson-Keasy and Keasy (1974) demonstrated that formal operations were necessary but not sufficient conditions for the emergence of principled moral reasoning. Nevertheless, Krebs and Gillmore (1982), in a study of children aged 5—14, and Haan et al. (1982), in a study of adolescents and adults, questioned the cognitive prerequisites hypothesis. Damon (1977), although he accepts the necessary-but-not-sufficient model, argues that this model does not imply any direct relationship between logical structure and moral thinking: it could be easier for an individual to use a moral concept than a different concept on the same logical level as the first one.

A report by Colby, Kohlberg, Gibbs, and Lieberman (1983), provides evidence for the Kohlbergian stage theory of moral development. They presented the results of a 20 year longitudinal study. They tested 58 boys, aged 10, 13, and 16 at the time when the original interview was administered, and continued with five follow-up interviews with 3—4 year intervals. It was shown that the proportion of positive to negative stage change was 14,75/1. Downward change was only 4% (6) of the adjacent testing times, but this was less than change on test-retest data, so downward change was attributed to measurement error. It was also shown that the subject did not reach a stage in the sequence without having gone through each preceding stage. Those results were interpreted as consistent with the hypothesis of invariant stage sequence. The hypothesis of stages as qualitatively different structural wholes was supported by the finding that the mean percentage of reasoning at the individual's stage proper was 67% and at the two most frequently used stages, which were always adjacent, was 99%. Factor analysis pointed to a general moral stage factor cutting across the three interview forms and the Standard Form Scoring Manual. Stage development was positively correlated with age. Furthermore, these results were not the same as earlier results: there was no evidence of stage six in this study.

In the same study, socio-economic status, education, and IQ were found to be positively correlated with moral judgment, but that did not affect the principles of the Kohlbergian cognitive developmental stage theory.

Some critical remarks

Kohlberg's theory (1969, 1976, 1981, 1984) is said to be a cognitive-developmental theory, a theory that belongs to cognitive psychology and that is influenced by Piaget. Kohlberg (1981), in his article "From Is to Ought: How to commit the naturalistic fallacy and get away with it in the study of moral development," outlines the philosophic structure of his theory. He takes a non-relativistic position, and he asserts that the sequence of moral development is universal and independent from culture:

> My account is based on a rejection of the relativity assumption and an acceptance of the contrasting view that "ethical principles" are the end point of a sequential "natural" development in social functioning and thinking; correspondingly, the stimulation of their development is a different matter from the inculcation of arbitrary cultural beliefs.
>
> (Kohlberg, 1981, p. 106)

This thesis is derived from the results of psychological empirical inquiry, and it is Kohlberg's conviction that philosophical "ought" statements have played a role in interaction with empirical psychological research. They have played that role, indeed.

In rejecting relativity, Kohlberg has argued against other theorists who claim that the development of social and moral thinking is defined as the direct internalization of cultural norms and values, e.g., learning theory and psychoanalysis. We may say that he is somehow right. It is very interesting for a psychologist to regard the underlying psychological processes, functions or mechanisms as distinct from their content, accept that distinction, and study them in interaction. Kohlberg's theory is such an attempt. Still, there is a danger in that. He can not avoid being influenced by the moral and political values of his society. In trying to derive "Ought" from "Is," Kohlberg is in fact deriving "Is" from the already existing "Ought" in a certain society. Therefore, Emler (1983a) has accused Kohlberg of having been influenced by individualism, rationalism, and liberalism, values that dominate the American ideology: the individual proceeds alone, independent from culture and society, through increasingly complex and adequate forms of reasoning caused purely by logical processes, to principled moral thinking, which emancipates him from the moral constraints imposed on him by society and state.

This emancipation from conventional thinking is at the same time the acceptance of the classical liberal values of justice and freedom. Similar critique has been directed towards Kohlberg by Baumrind (1978). Kohlberg himself says that the concept of justice at stage 6 is based on the principles of liberty and equality as they are expressed in the U.S. Constitution (Kohlberg, 1985, p. 37).

Kohlberg's theory is influenced very much by Piaget's theory of genetic epistemology. Nevertheless, there are some doubts about the affinity of the two theories. At first glance, Kohlberg's theory seems to be a more sophisticated Piagetian theory in the area of moral development. However, a closer look reveals a difference in a very important aspect. Piaget's theory is first of all a constructivistic theory. That means that the individual's moral structures are constructed by him while he is acting upon the social world he lives in. It is unlikely that this process can lead to universal modes of moral thinking, because as the social conditions and relations vary in different cultures, so do action and thinking. That means that it is unlikely to achieve Kohlbergian universality, in contrast to Spinozian universality. The latter is not implying the discovery of some kind of universal moral content through universal processes. Instead of that, the Spinozian universality is constructed through logical and scientific processes, the adoption of which are necessary in order to serve the true nature of man. Still, Kohlberg asserts that the development of moral thinking unfolds through universal sequence which leads to stage six, i.e., the discovery of the principle of justice (a hypothesis that he did not find empirical support for). Such a theory can not be compatible with constructivism. Although Kohlberg (Kohlberg & Candee, 1984b) stresses the formal features of moral judgment such as universability, prescriptivity, reversibility, and generality, he can not avoid the accusation of being an ethical realist, i.e., the view that there are existing autonomous moral principles which one has to discover, and according to which one has to live (Vine, 1983).

On the other hand, it is not always necessary to be an ethical realist in order to avoid ethical relativism if you are not a Kohlbergian theorist. Indeed, relativism is not incompatible with the Kohlbergian formal features of moral judgment. That means that the content of the principle of justice can be substituted with some other content, while judgments and actions continue to be consistent with this new content, i.e., the same formal features are found in the new content. Then, only a recourse to realism can serve as a safeguard against absolute relativism. The Piagetian theory does not face such a problem. In being forced to adapt to the social world, the individual has to take into consideration both his nature and the factors in the world outside. Consequently, unlimited variations of the resulting moral concepts and principles are impossible, since, at least, the core of the human nature is not supposed to vary freely.

Kohlberg's rationalism and ethical realism have some implications for the thought-action problem. First, his theory is concerned with knowing and not with acting. Consequently, he is very close to the Platonic view that he who knows the right thing, acts according to it. Secondly, there are some problems when the dilemma-reasoning subjects try to act according to their thinking (Blasi, 1980,1983). Kohlberg tried to bridge the gap by inducing first the notion of ego-strength, and later the theory that the higher-stage subjects are more consistent in their actions, by differentiating between deontic and responsibility judgments.

Most recently Kohlberg introduced the division of the stages into two substages: type A and type B (Kohlberg & Candee, 1984a & 1984b; Kohlberg, Higgins, Tappan & Schrader, 1984; see also Gibbs et al., 1986). Piaget's theory focuses on the relationship between thought and action. His method investigates the evolutional process of an unconscious act to a conscious one. Kohlberg's proposal of the two types aims to provide a solution to the thought-action problem by using a part of these ideas of Piaget. He attempts to find out the typology of Piaget's two phases of moral development: the heteronomous and autonomous phases. Although Piaget did not differentiate between these phases in the same way as Kohlberg does, Kohlberg identifies type A with heteronomy and type B with autonomy. Furthermore, he supposes that the actions of the type B individual, at a stage, are more consistent with his moral thinking than the actions of a type A individual.

Kohlberg defines the difference between these two types as a difference in characteristics, content, and structure, or as a mixture of them. Still, in trying to explain the thought-action phenomena by reference to a part of the Piagetian theory, he indirectly accepts the two phases of production of moral knowledge which are independent from the Kohlbergian characteristics, content, and structure of moral thinking. More important, he admits that a significant difference exists between him and Piaget with regard to the problems they are interested in solving with their theories.

That difference lies in the definition of development. Piaget understands development as the formation of autonomous conscious thinking, whereas Kohlberg's interest lies in the discovery of universal principles. Inherent in Piaget's thinking is the notion of a never ending adaptive process of constructing new structures of moral thinking. On the other hand, Kohlberg states explicitly that the process of moral development is given. Although that view is undoubtedly different from Piaget, in form it bears more relationship to Piaget's general theory of cognitive development (Piaget, 1936; Piaget & Inhelder, 1969; Brainerd, 1978) than to his moral theory (Piaget, 1932), or to his later publications about the general theory (Piaget, 1976, 1978, 1980). Kohlberg has given a picture of man as a discoverer of fixed principles which he has to follow strictly. There is no place for independent thinking and action. What is development then? Is it reasoning and acting according to higher (more abstract) principles, or the emancipation from certain values and the formation of new more adaptive ones? We may assume that the latter, the Piagetian view, provides a better answer to that question, since, at least, the first answer seems to be included in the second.

It must also be said that Piaget's general cognitive theory describes processes of operations which produce knowledge. On the contrary, Kohlberg's moral reasoning at each stage can hardly produce any new knowledge. The individual has only to follow an imperative, which is different at each stage. The focus of the Kohlbergian research is on the description of the different forms thought follows in appealing to these imperatives of moral principles.

Kurtines and Greif (1974) have criticized the studies which provide support for Kohlberg's theory as not having tested it adequately. They asserted that the Moral Judgment Scale lacked standardization of both administration and scoring, that there had been no great interest in estimating the reliability of the Scale, that the predictive and construct validity are minimal, and that there was evidence suggesting a different explanation of the moral phenomena than Kohlberg's. Broughton (1978), in a reply to them, accepted some of the critique, but he stated that they had misinterpreted the theory as being a psychometric model.

Other criticisms from inside Kohlbergian tradition come from Gilligan (1977). She found that there is a difference between the sexes in moral reasoning. Women tend to focus more on responsibility, whereas men focus more on rights and rules. A study by Gibbs et al. (1984) provided support for Gilligan's claim.

Gibbs (1977, 1979) offers a different interpretation of the stage sequence. He distinguishes between naturalistic and existential themes in psychology, and he argues that the first four stages meet the naturalistic criteria, i.e., provide answers to the question "how," whereas the principled stages 5 and 6 provide answers to existential questions.

Bergling (1981), in his integrated review and examination of the Kohlbergian approach, found that several hypotheses had been rejected or partly rejected. Also Snarey (1985) criticized the hypothesis of cross-cultural universality for stage 5. He concluded that this higher stage does not account for moral reasoning involving principles that dominate non-western cultures.

However, Kohlberg's theory is broadly accepted: (a) because of its tremendous empirical support, and (b) because it offers a theory of the development of the concrete and limited moral thinking towards abstract and broader thinking. This may not only be interpreted in a Platonic-idealistic sense, as Kohlberg does, but it may be accepted as an innate tendency (Chomsky, 1980), or as a consequence of the development towards a more adaptive and functional thinking in terms of Piaget and Vygotsky. The direction of the concrete-abstract dimension of development is plausible, as it is broadly acknowledged. On the other hand, there is a dimension that Kohlberg assumes does not undergo any development. In arguing against relativism, in his study he has tried to integrate psychological processes with morality in society. However, he did not succeed in discerning the real relationship between the psychological function and culture. A society may impose abstract thinking. Indeed, western society does it. Usually, the conditions in industrialized society force the individual to think more abstractly than in other societies. But, the most important factor contributing to the imposition of abstract thinking is probably the long and compulsory education which every child receives in the western societies. That could imply that Kohlberg's theory is relativistic or culture dependent, when at the same time it is known from empirical studies that in some cultures no principled thinking exists. Of course, we may acknowledge the Kohlbergian contribution of development towards abstract thinking in the sense that such thinking is both demanded and imposed by a certain society. Still, judging and acting according to abstract principles does not imply any development of the productive thought processes, but only an adaptation of the content of thought to social reality. This adaptation may be obtained either through automatic acceptance (imposition by culture and importation by the individual) or by independent, active, and scientific search. Kohlberg says nothing about this issue, and he does not differentiate between these two modes of acquisition of moral concepts or principles. On the contrary, Piaget has offered a theory of the process of becoming independent from cultural imposition or constraint.

It is very interesting then to study the structure of thinking in relation to the existence or non-existence of the content of cultural moral knowledge. It is not interesting for us, in the investigation of thought development, to study the dimension of its content (concrete-abstract or pre-, postconventional) or its deeper structure (the Kohlbergian structure or scheme), but the dimension of its mode of function, i.e., the development of thinking from an automatic to a conscious-scientific phase and how it is advanced or regressed by the functionality of the imposed moral cultural content, which is based on Piaget's theory.

Intervention and education

Whereas Kohlbergian research was primarily focused on the description of the characteristics of stage development, its sequentiality, its hierarchy, and its relationship to age, Turiel, who also belongs to the same tradition, has directed his research towards the processes underlying stage transition. The main assumption he makes, as Kohlberg does, is that development from a lower to a higher stage in the Kohlbergian scale is caused by disequilibrium:

> It is disequilibrium, which is characterized by conceptions of inadequacies, contradictions, and inconsistencies in the existing way of thinking, that can result in activities producing new information leading to the reorganization of thought. If the child's existing way of thinking inadequately handles encountered events, the result may be disequilibrium that can precipitate a gradual process of reorganization into a form of thought that more adequately coordinates the child's previous conceptions with the novel, discrepant events.
>
> (Turiel, 1983, p. 20)

This assumption is influenced by Piaget's disequilibrium hypothesis as the driving force underlying intellectual development. Turiel accepted this and started to study sequentiality and hierarchy of stages through the investigation of stage preference. In an earlier study (Turiel, 1966) he observed that subjects at stages 2, 3, and 4 were influenced by the presentation of moral reasoning higher or lower than their own. Precisely, it indicated that one-stage-above treatment was more effective than the two-stages-above or the one-below. These facts were interpreted as supporting the Kohlbergian theory, but most important, they showed that it was possible to influence the process of moral development. Of course, this influence was hypothesized to exist inside the Kohlbergian frame, i.e., it is only the rate of development that is affected by the presentation of the one-stage-above reasoning. The same results were obtained in another study made by Rest, Turiel, and Kohlberg (1969). Children's rejection of the lower stage advice was due to its structural-developmental characteristics and the assimilation of the higher-level advice was due to the preference factor rather than the comprehension factor. On the contrary, the failure to assimilate the two-stage-above reasoning was caused by the children's inability to comprehend its structure. This differentiation between comprehension and preference, or content and structure, provided an explanation for the phenomenon of non-existence of stage 6 reasoners despite the abundant presence of principled reasoning in society. Leaders speak and write in a principled mode; constitutions and different proclamations are written in the same way. Nevertheless, people may comprehend the content and assimilate it because it supports their opinion, but they fail to grasp the structure of principled reasoning. The assimilation of content does not cause any structural contradiction, and modeling alone can not lead to stage transition. Progression on the developmental scale is achieved only through the presentation of some form of structural conflict, combined with the degree of stage mixture (Turiel, 1969).

Although it is possible to influence the rate of stage transition by the initiation of a cognitive-structural conflict through the presentation of higher order reasoning, it was observed that its effect was not the same at different stages of moral development. In an experiment, inspired by Milgram's (1963) famous obedience study, Turiel and Rothman (1972) examined the effects of exposure to moral reasoning on behavioral choices. It is important to emphasize that this study, despite the tradition of Kohlberg's pure, rationalistic method, introduced behavioral response as a dependent variable. As in Milgram's study, it was found that subjects tend to continue to punish the complaining "learner." When presented with reasoning at the stage above or below their own, subjects at stages 2 and 3 persisted in this choice. Stage 4 subjects, however, shifted when the reasoning supporting the choice to stop was at the stage above. This difference in influence was explained as an effect of the stage 4 subjects' competence to integrate the higher order reasoning with their own behavioral choice. They subordinated the behavior to reasoning so the assimilation of the higher-stage reasoning influenced their behavior. In contrast, stage 2 and 3 subjects kept the two domains segregated, so they failed to subordinate their behavioral choice to the more advanced reasoning.

Later, Turiel (1974, 1977) attempted a closer analysis of the transitional process from lower to higher stages. It was observed that the high school subjects usually categorized as stage 4 reasoners, showed a tendency to regress to stage 2. This was explained as caused by social pressure and rendered temporal status (Kohlberg & Kramer, 1969). Turiel disagreed with that interpretation and argued that what appears to be stage 2 reasoning in fact only resembles it in content but actually represents a structure higher than stage 4. The transitional stage $4\frac{1}{2}$ was discovered. The main characteristic of stage $4\frac{1}{2}$ is that the individual is involved in a phase of disequilibrium: he rejects the validity of making moral judgments or using any moral terminology, when he actually makes moral judgments and uses moral terminology. It is mainly a conflict between relativism and moralism, reflecting an incomplete understanding of stage 5 structure and a rejection of stage 4 reasoning. Equilibrium then is obtained through the differentiation between the conventional and the moral, i.e., the relativistic thinking about the first domain and the formulation of a new principled conception of morality concerning what belongs to the second domain. That differentiation implies also an integration of the whole moral and social thinking. Turiel and his associate Nucci continued to study those two domains of social knowledge (Nucci & Turiel, 1978; Nucci,

1981; Nucci & Nucci, 1982a, 1982b; Turiel, 1983).

In conclusion, Turiel's research on the transitional process may be regarded as having provided evidence for the influence assumption. Namely, it is now possible to hypothesize that there must be some way to intervene in the developmental process of moral thinking. If we construct a suitable method of instruction, we can influence moral development or at least its rate. Additionally, Turiel and Rothman's study showed that even behavior choice may be shifted as a result of higher stage advice. That is the main contribution of Turiel's research, besides the explanation it gives to the fact of people's non-assimilation of stage 6 reasoning.

On the other hand, that notion of influence belongs to Kohlbergian theorizing. It is supposed to have effect only on the transition from a lower to a higher stage on Kohlberg's stage scale, and on the developmental process from concrete to abstract thinking. That developmental dimension denotes the theory's rationalism. The disequilibrium is not caused by the individual's interaction with reality but purely through a cognitive conflict. Therefore, the developmental process is not supposed to have any functional dimension. The distinction between content and structure is understood only as a certain stage's content and structure, and it is adopted in order to explain the isolated cognitive conflict. Structure does not mean the underlying organization or hierarchy of the cognitive knowledge producing processes, but rather a kind of content, which is more general, more stable, and deeper, the Kohlbergian scheme, i.e., the structure of the content. The every day cognitive function is understood as the production of thoughts patterned after the underlying structure, which may be called internal heteronomy. Even the notion of responsibility, adopted as an answer to the thought-action problem, emphasizes the theory's focus on the ways of following the moral principles rather than the producing processes of moral knowledge. According to Kohlberg, the every day cognitive function is not a way (automatic or scientific) of production of the cognitive content and its structure. Structural changes occur by jumping from stage to stage, but this mode of change, besides being rational (not caused by a confrontation with reality), seems to be an automatic process that does not demand man's consciousness and logical reason in order for that change to occur. Kohlberg's theory gives us no chance to study independent, logical, and scientific, versus automatic and heteronomous thinking in a meaningful social setting for the individual, despite his important contribution to the theory of moral development.

Recently, Kohlberg approached the issue of moral education in a different way. He studied the influence of the moral atmosphere of the school upon the formation and obedience to new rules. Indeed, he found significant differences between the democratic and the traditional schools. The results showed that the students in the democratic schools rated higher than the traditional high school students in their judgments concerning hypothetical as well as practical dilemmas; they showed a higher frequency of responsibility judgments and pro-social choice for self and others. Furthermore, the students in the democratic schools possessed a higher degree of the collectiveness of norms and of community valuing, such as a higher phase of the collective norm (Higgins et al., 1984; Kohlberg, 1985).

What is interesting about the democratic school is not only the acquisition of these characteristics, but also the formation of new rules in that "just community." The moral atmosphere of the group is very important for the establishment of equality and cooperation among the individual members. Still the understanding of the spirit and the aims of the community, as well as the intervention by an instructor are necessary for the formation of new, more functional rules.

> . . . my role in community meetings, and the role which I strove to teach the staff, was to speak not for myself but as representing the spirit, traditions and future of the community. In this spirit I would (1) advocate making a rule or developing a collective norm important to the school and (2) attempt to tie this norm to the welfare and spirit of community of the group.
>
> (Kohlberg, 1985, p. 46)

That spirit is understood as the nucleus of a special community, the deeper cause of the construction of this community, and the aim of its existence. Thus the main problems that a community or a social group encounters are related to that spirit. Consequently the understanding of this relationship by the members of the group or community is necessary in order to find the most functional solutions to these problems by the formulation and acceptance of appropriate rules.

It is obvious then that this later Kohlbergian mode of thinking approaches Piaget. First and foremost, the introduction of the problematique of the formulation of new moral rules, but also the significance of moral atmosphere, i.e., equality and cooperation, and the role played by a "collaborator," are sufficient to show this new Kohlbergian tendency.

Indeed, the most important aspect of this turn is the theory that the creation of disequilibrium, which is necessary for the formulation of new moral rules by cooperating individuals in a democratic/equal community, is possible through pointing to the spirit of that same community by a collaborator/instructor, and the subsequent understanding of that by the members of the community.

Yet, this tardy approach to the essential Piaget does not imply any rejection of the Kohlbergian theory accepted up to that time. Kohlberg is still interested in the stage advancement of morality. He focuses his research on the characteristics of this stage development and on the stages of the individual moral reasoning and valuing of norms and community. He is interested primarily in the features of community where the formulation of new rules is taking place, and not on the formulation process itself. It seems that the formulation process is used only as a mean for the understanding and explanation of the stage characteristics of moral thinking and community. Piaget, on the contrary, is primarily interested in the formulation process itself, whereas the characteristics of this process have a secondary value. Consequently, the issue of planned instruction is not important for Kohlberg.

Although Kohlberg mentions the spirit of the community as a very important factor for the formulation of new moral rules, the stage development which he presents does not lead to a principle of justice (representing the spirit of the community) as Piaget understands it, but to the high, abstract and rational Kohlbergian "Justice."

Kohlberg's (1984) distinction between A and B substages and between deontic and responsibility judgments, such as his interest in the moral atmosphere and the just community, are indeed approaches to Piaget, although his aim is only to provide an answer to the thought-action problem. The weakness of his theory on this issue forced him to adopt the problematique of the formulation of moral rules by the adapted and functional moral thinking processes of cooperating individuals. He accepted even the positive influence of a collaborator. Nevertheless, Kohlberg does not abandon his theory which continues to focus its research on the description of the features of the stage development of moral thinking towards the rational principle of Justice.

Also worth mentioning is the work of William Damon, who takes a stand closer to that of Piaget, although he is influenced by the Kohlbergian theory of stage development.

Damon (1977) does not accept the Kohlbergian method of studying moral development, since that model is in reality investigating children's responses to moral problems that are derived from the adult world. Consequently, the dilemmas may be meaningless for the children. On the contrary, he prefers to use the Piagetian method because it allows the study of the special social world of the child, which is distinct from adult morality.

This second approach focuses on behaviors that serve the same *function* throughout the course of development, rather than (as in the first approach) on behaviors that are assumed to be connected developmentally. By "function" is meant the general adaptive purpose to which the behavior is directed. . . . Piaget's (1932) investigation into early morality is an example of the second approach in action and provides us with a good contrast to Kohlberg's use of methodology.

(Damon, 1977, pp. 40—41)

Although Damon tries to use a method that is not purely hypothetical and rationalistic, he does not succeed in avoiding the influence of the Kohlbergian tradition. Not only does his theory describe the child's development of positive justice and authority conceptions as unfolding through six different levels (which have much in common with Kohlberg's stages), but, his work also aims to provide just a description of moral functioning and not the formation of autonomous thinking.

On the other hand, Damon's work, indeed, supports some parts of Piaget's theory. In a study of the relationship of positive justice conceptions to logical operations, he found that there was a strong association between the two. That did not mean, however, that logico-mathematical thinking was a necessary condition for the development of moral thinking (Damon, 1975). Although he presupposes some kind of general structure or organizing principles underlying moral thinking, he does not regard development as going through distinct and general stages:

> . . . we assume that the general structure appears in a number of manifestations and that the child's attainment of it in one manifestation makes likely, but not certain, his attainment of it in another.
>
> (Damon, 1977, p. 323)

and he concludes that:

> . . . we have chosen to refrain from drawing conclusions about the stagelike development of social knowledge in children.
>
> (Damon, 1977, p. 343)

Damon came to the same conclusion later (1980) in a longitudinal study of the patterns of change in children's social reasoning. The results showed that the development towards higher levels proceeded gradually with considerable continuity in the child's moral thinking. Before a transition occurred to the next higher level it was found that reasoning similar to the higher level was present on the predominant level.

Cooperation, also, was found to be a very important condition for the moral development (Damon & Killen, 1982). Children who participated in discussion groups with their peers were more likely to advance in their moral reasoning than were children who participated in discussions only with adults. This is in line with Piaget's (1932) thesis as well as with Kohlberg's (1985) moral education theory. Thus, Damon comes to the conclusion that there are some conditions for cooperation which influence the advance of moral development. Children who participated in the briefer groups tended to change their moral reasoning progressively in comparison with children who participated in the longer groups. Groups that were dominated by conflicts between the children were not so successful in initiating change. Rather, it was hypothesized that development owed its advance to reciprocity in a group.

32

Concerning the thought-action problem, Damon takes a position closer to Kohlberg (Damon, 1984; Damon & Hart, 1982). He showed that the conceptual systems of self and morality, which are uncoordinated during childhood, became integrated as the child grows to an adolescent. That implies that the adolescent who regards morality as central to his self-identity is more prepared for moral action than a younger child. Damon offers a description of the characteristics of the relationship of self-understanding to moral principles, which imply that the younger child focuses on his physical and active self, whereas the adolescent describes himself more in social and psychological terms with a strong relationship to moral principles.

INTERNALIZATION AND LEARNING THEORY

Although Kohlberg did not focus his research on the issue of the influence of intervention or instruction upon moral development, during the 1960's, learning theorists directed their interest towards the mechanisms of internalization. Bandura and Aronfreed tried to offer explanations consistent with learning theory to the phenomena of children's acquisition of moral behavior.

Bandura and McDonald (1963) studied the behavior of children in the two Piagetian phases under the influence of social reinforcement and modeling. Their hypothesis was that modeling and social reinforcement would produce changes in the children's behavior even "downwards," i.e., from subjective moral judgment to objective moral judgment. The results confirmed the hypothesis and showed that modeling and reinforcement play an important role in the internalization process.

Despite these results, their conclusion that change may be possible in every direction, came into question in a replication of their study by Cowan et al. (1969). They showed that the effects of modeling and reinforcement do not remain after a longer period (2 weeks) in the moving-down-condition, but that the treatment has a continued effect in the case of the moving-up-condition.

In discussing the Atayals, a Malaysian aboriginal group on Formosa, Kohlberg (1969) says that adolescents, living in a society which believes that dreams are real, experience a conflict when they come to discover that what they have dreamed the previous night was not real. This leads to a kind of regressive learning which is not isolated in the area of social learning, but expands its effects to children's other natural beliefs. At the age of 11—15, when dream regression takes place, children partially lose conservation. Other studies (Turiel, 1966; Rest et al., 1969) showed that it was much easier for a child to learn the stage above than the stage below his own.

Despite the conflict between Bandura and Kohlberg, we may say Bandura (1969; Bandura & McDonald, 1963) has pointed out the role played by modeling and consequences, as a way of thinking and behavior to be internalized by the child. This is ignored, especially by Piaget, who is interested in the passing from autonomy to heteronomy. In turn this Piagetian transformation of existing thinking through action to conscious thinking is, of course, outside Bandura's interests.

The issue of advancing and/or regressing in moral thinking, such as posed by Kohlberg and collaborators, is not essential. An individual may have the flexibility to pass from subjective responsibility to objective responsibility answers in a judgment situation. Nevertheless, this can not be a verdict for a definitive switch to a lower stage. If one takes into account the consequences, it may be natural for one to judge in accordance with the principle of objective responsibility. This means that we can not exclude the possibility that one has decided to change his mode of thinking autonomously and critically. The point here is that the advance or the regression is not an indication of change in the heteronomy-autonomy dimension. What Bandura's and McDonald's study has shown is that modeling and reinforcement are effective methods of inducing ways of thinking and judging in children. Still, this is heteronomous thinking.

Bandura's work (1969, 1977) is an attempt to describe the underlying learning mechanisms of social behavior. He presupposes some internal representational processes which mediate subsequent behavioral reproduction of modeling stimuli. This internal representation is not intended to be a kind of structural developmental change in the mind of the child; rather it depends on circumstances.

The work of Aronfreed (1969, 1976), on the other hand, tries to give a more stable explanation of the internalization. Of course, his work does not override the limits of the learning theory tradition. In a series of studies (Aronfreed, 1961, 1963; Aronfreed, Cutick & Fagen, 1963; Aronfreed & Reber, 1965), Aronfreed showed that, although the child's social behavior is controlled in the beginning by external contingencies, it is gradually governed by internal control that represents the functions of the external contingencies.

The typical experiment contained a treatment situation in which high versus low cognitive structure was used by the experimenter to describe the child's responsibility, i.e., to provide standards of evaluation, and a test situation where the experimenter prompted the child to produce self-critical or reparative responses to a transgression.

The results indicated clearly that cognitive structure was the main inducing factor for internalization of responsibility. The same results were obtained in Aronfreed's (1961) research on moral judgments made by children who came from different social classes. Working class children were more prone to focus on external responsibility, whereas middle class children were self-critical. This was explained by the fact that working class mothers used disciplinary techniques which put emphasis on mother's punitive presence, in contrast to middle class mother's, who used methods which induced in the child reactions to his own transgressions; these reactions could become independent of their original external stimulus sources.

The learning mechanism underlying internalization is a kind of conditioned tranquilizing effect. Aronfreed maintains that any act of transgression is always followed by social punishment to suppress that act. This punishment produces anxiety which becomes attached to some intrinsic stimuli of the transgressive act. These stimuli may be produced by the initiation of the performance of the act itself or by the cognitive or verbal representations of this performance. The suppression of the act, since it is punished by external social agents, eliminates the intrinsic stimuli of the act and attenuates the anxiety which has been attached to these stimuli. The punishment-produced anxiety, such as its reduction for the suppression of the act, is now moved from its actual performance and its cognitive representation to its intrinsic stimulus correlates. It is internalized and independent of external consequences.

Aronfreed's internalization thesis, consistent with learning theory, does not imply any structural or developmental change in the child's social and moral thinking and behavior. Yet, his approach offers some more permanent explanation of these phenomena than Bandura's does.

The role played by the level of cognitive structure in order to internalize any moral behavior is very important. It is an area that Piaget (1932) did not study systematically, although he mentioned it on almost every page of his book as "adult constraint." Both Bandura and Aronfreed were pioneers in studying the influence of external factors on changing moral thinking and behavior. Nevertheless, their research leads to a dead end. They study the influence of the outside world through the classical principles of learning theory, and they not only accept, but as Aronfreed, they advocate a cognitive representation. Still, this is meant to be an unconscious representation. It is a representation which can not be used for critical planning and change, for such thinking is not supposed to exist. It is produced and changed by automatic learning mechanisms.

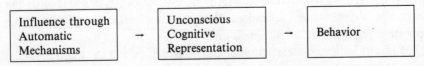

Fig 1. A model for the theories of Bandura and Aronfreed.

This conceptual model (Fig 1) is different from Piaget's theory. While Piaget overlooks the role of the external influence, Bandura and Aronfreed show its importance. Still, the fundamental difference between these theories is the focus of the interest. Piaget is interested in the formation of autonomous, critical and scientific thinking, while Bandura's and Aronfreed's theoretical framework does not allow an expansion to this area of research.

36

PIAGET'S THEORY OF MORAL DEVELOPMENT

The study of the autonomous moral thinking

Piaget was one of the first scientists who approached the area of moral development. His book *"The moral judgment of the child"* (1932; see even Piaget, 1972) became a classic and has inspired a considerable amount of research since then. In studying this early work we can discern the grounds of the Piagetian theoretical principles and research method. Although this is the ground on which Kohlberg tried to build his theory, there are some essential differences between them. Piaget reveals himself as the scientist who endeavours to establish a theory of the liberation of man from ideological oppression, whereas Kohlberg attempts only to describe the outcomes or the characteristics of a developmental process. Kohlberg's theory is static in contrast to Piaget's dynamic theory:

> The one thing we have to remember is that in the psychology of norms the successive stages is not everything: the direction itself, the *vector*, . . ., counts for more than anything else.
>
> (Piaget, 1932, p. 392)

Piaget studied, in different experiments, children's thought and action development on (1) the rules of the game, (2) lying and responsibility, and (3) punishment and justice.

In studying the development of children's thinking and action about rules, Piaget observed children when they played the game of marbles, a very common game among children at that time in Switzerland. He focused on the following of the rules in practice and asked them to describe for him the rules, to tell him who created the rules, for how long they have existed, and if they could invent new rules.

The results showed that there are four stages in the development of the practice of the game and three stages in regard to the consciousness of the rules. The first stage is only motoric and individual in character. The child at an early age handles the marbles as he desires following only his motor habits. In handling these objects the child understands the objects' nature and adapts his motor schemes to the situation. Slowly, these acts become schematized and ritualized, and the marbles become symbols. Although this ritualism is the origin of the rules, it does not yet imply any consciousness about them.

Later, at the age of 3—6 years, the egocentric child has established a relationship to other children. He does not play alone any more, so his previous acquired ritualized acts can be approved of or enjoined. This social interaction gives the child a sense of obligation which is necessary for the formation of consciousness. Of course, this relationship to other children is not yet mutual and cooperative. It has a dual character. The child imitates the older children's rule-governed play, but he uses the examples he receives in a purely individual manner. He thinks that he uses the same rules when in reality he changes them as he wishes, unaware of his social isolation. In spite of that, his consciousness regards rules as sacred and untouchable. They are supposed to be eternal and divine, created by a great authority. Therefore, children do not accept any suggestion to change them, because they think that any intervention is going to damage them and that it is impossible to improve them. This is the heteronomy condition (Table 1).

When the child grows older, at 7—10 years, his consciousness and practice concerning the rules changes: he does not regard them as untouchable anymore, although he now tries to follow them in detail. This new cooperation condition together with the later codification of rules (11—12 years) constitute the autonomous phase of moral development. Now the child begins to play the game in a condition of mutual control and practices the rules correctly. In a later phase within the autonomy condition the child comes to understand the meaning of the game, and he is ready to improve the rules or invent new ones, in cooperation with his peers, in order to make the game more interesting (Table 1).

These two qualitatively different functions of moral life were found by Piaget in other areas of children's action and thinking as well. In order to study children's conceptions about lying, Piaget told them hypothetical stories about children who lied, and he asked them to judge those transgressions. The younger children relied in their judgments on the material damage caused by the lie and looked at differences between the lie and the truth. The more serious the material damage was and the greater the difference was between the lie and the truth, the more severe the judgment was. Children did not take into consideration the liar's intention. They also judged a lie as more serious if it was told to an adult rather than to a child, and if the liar was punished for that. Those judgments were not made by older children. In autonomy they took into their mind the liar's intention rather than the material damage and thought that the successful lie was more serious than that which failed to be credible (Table 1).

The same results were found with regard to responsibility. In the

Table 1. The predominant characteristics of moral thinking in Heteronomy vs. Autonomy, according to Piaget.

	Heteronomy	Autonomy
Rules:	Unchangeable, Eternal	Improvement, Invention by Agreement
Lying:	Objective Consequences Amount of Punishment	Intention, Mutual Trust, Affection
Responsibility:	Objective, Extent of Damage	Subjective, Motives, Intention
Punishment:	Expiatory, Retributive "Immanent Justice"	Preventive, Educative, Reciprocal
Justice:	Defined by Adult Authority	Equality in Relativity, Reciprocity

heteronomy condition, children thought that the delinquent's responsibility had a proportional relationship to the extent of material damage, whereas in their judgment autonomous children relied on subjective factors such as intention and motives (Table 1).

Children's conceptions of punishment were different in the phases of autonomy and heteronomy. Heteronomous children thought that punishment was right as expiation and as a kind of retribution to the agent of a transgression. Therefore, punishment should be given as a kind of revenge, and the punishment's amount should be proportionate to the magnitude of the damage caused by the transgression. On the other hand, autonomous children preferred punishment that had an educative role. They were much more interested in using punishment in order to prevent future delinquencies and to maintain the reciprocity and solidarity among the individuals in a cooperation setting (Table 1).

Also, the concept of justice, i.e., the principle of distribution of a reinforcement or a punishment among the members of a group, undergoes such a development from the heteronomy to the autonomy phase. In the beginning children relied purely on adult authority. They accepted the way adults distributed the reinforcement as the only right, however it was given. There were no unjust reinforcements and punishments if they were given by the adult; everything that was reinforced was right, and everything that was punished was wrong. Later when children grew up and began to practice cooperation, they discarded adult authority as the source of justice and demanded identical equality. Everybody in the group should receive exactly the same amount of what was given, despite the differences of its members. This development did not culminate until the age of 12. From that age children took into account the differences in the group, the contribution and the vulnerability of each member, and the coincidences. The principle of justice was then equality in relativity (Table 1).

Constraint and instruction

The results of this study led Piaget to conclude that there were two distinct moral functions of the child:

> . . . it is desirable, so it seems to us, to establish a difference in kind between unilateral respect, which leads to the recognition of heteronomous norms, and the mutual respect, which recognizes no law but its own mutualness and which leads to the formation of norms that function within itself.
>
> (Piaget, 1932, p. 390)

Those two different functions of the moral conduct of the child have often been misinterpreted as two general stages of development. In turn, this view has been criticized because no empirical support was found for that (Bergling, 1982). Of course, Piaget himself has never asserted that the issue is about two integrated general stages which characterize the psychical function of the child. The autonomous function in regard to a moral area is not supposed to imply that the child thinks and acts autonomously in other areas as well.

> There are therefore no inclusive stages which define the whole of a subject's mental life at a given point of his evolution; the stages should be thought of as the successive phases of regular processes recurring like a rythm on the superposed planes of behavior and consciousness. A given individual, may for example, have reached the stage of autonomy with regard to a certain group of rules, while his consciousness, together with the practice of certain more stable rules, will still be coloured with heteronomy. We can not therefore speak of global or inclusive stages characterized as such by autonomy or heteronomy, but only of phases of heteronomy or autonomy which define a process that is repeated for each new set of rules or for each new plane of thought or reflection.
>
> (Piaget, 1932, pp. 78—79)

> We see, therefore, how the spontaneous realism of the early years, while it dwindles progressively with regard to the subject's own conduct, may very well develop elsewhere, first in the evaluation of other people's actions, and finally in reflection concerning purely theoretical cases . . .
>
> (Piaget, 1932, p. 182)

We can see then that, although there are two different moral functions, they do not constitute two distinct general stages that form structural wholes. In this sense, Piaget's theory is different from Kohlberg's (Emler, 1983b).

In our previous discussion about the relationship between Kohlberg and

Piaget we have seen that the former tries to explain what it is that distinguishes his theory from other socialization theories. He says that his theory is a cognitive one which means that it postulates a representational or coding process intervening between stimulus and response. However, these representations are not learned in the sense that Baldwin or learning theories mean. He asserts that his theory is based on Piaget's assumption of disequilibrium as the process underlying the development of the cognitive structures.

Kohlberg (1969) says that: ". . . cognitive structures are always structures (schemata) of action" (p. 348). Of course, this is a Piagetian thesis, too. Still, one can not avoid remarking that such a view implies that through the whole cognitive development, in all stages, there is only one dominating underlying structure: the structure of action. If principled moral thinking like the preconventional moral thinking are structures of action, what is meant by development to Kohlberg? It does not indicate a development of the underlying cognitive structure, because this always remains the same. It is only the content, the equilibrated product or the characteristic of the structure of action, which is different at different stages. From a Kohlbergian perspective development is seen as the movement to more abstract and inclusive imperatives to reason morally.

Piaget describes moral development as going through two phases, while Kohlberg offers a six stage/three level theory. The question is if such a theory would be able to describe the most interesting underlying psychological function in relation to external influence like heteronomy versus autonomy, or if it could only describe the most salient characteristics and content of moral thinking.

Kohlberg (1969, p. 349) writes that: "All the basic processes involved in 'physical' cognitions, and in stimulating developmental changes in these cognitions, are also basic to social development." That means that there is no difference between physical and moral cognition. Kohlberg points to that in order to show that his stage theory corresponds to Piaget's operational stages about the physical world. As we have previously seen, Piaget's stages are processes of solving problems and not only the results of them, as in the case of Kohlbergian stages. Piaget's stages describe ways of thinking and action, and not the dominating concepts of reasoning of the child at different stages.

Nevertheless, it would be somewhat difficult even for Piaget to claim that the development proceeds through general and distinct stages. In fact, even his theory, like Kohlberg's theory, postulates structures of action which become more and more abstract and formal. Consequently, this does not imply any qualitative different kind of thinking at each of the various hypothesized stages of operational thinking about physical reality. Also, the logical deficiencies of the stage hypothesis and generally of the constructivist theory have been discussed by Chomsky (1980).

Obviously, the notion of development does not point to stages and stage transition, but to the movement towards more abstract operations in order to adapt to reality. It is the process of being conscious. This is the main contribution of Piaget's later work (1976, 1978, 1980). His early work on moral development has also contributed to that, but that work was connected with another very important factor: the influence from the outside world upon that process of becoming conscious. In short, neither Piaget's later work on consciousness about physical reality, nor his early work on moral development seems to postulate stages (see even Damon, 1977). Kohlberg's theory, on the other hand, is not compatible with the stage hypothesis in regard to action schemata, but only as a description of the fixed products of the equilibration process.

Another very important aspect of the Piagetian theory is the issue of the time lag between the successful practice of an action and the conscious realization of that. Piaget writes that:

Thought always lags behind action and cooperation has to be practiced for a very long time before its consequences can be brought fully to light by reflective thought.

(Piaget, 1932, p. 56)

That is the well-known Piagetian thesis that the performance of an act does not imply that this is conscious for the child. Rather, the problems that arise during the practice or action and the discrepancies between the thought about the action and the actual action itself, cause disequilibrium, which leads to reflection on the inadequate thought. The child then becomes conscious, and he is able to master that previously unconscious thought. Therefore, it is very important to underline the fact, accepted by Piaget, of the existence of some thinking before and during an act, although it is not conscious and not in accordance with the action it attempts to guide and describe. In the 1932 study, Piaget, not only accepts that, but he describes its features in detail. It is the heteronomous moral thinking with moral realism, objective responsibility, immanent justice, and unchangeable social rules. Moreover, it is thinking that only exists in an unconscious form, and it is internalized by children from adult authority.

The child has to free himself from adult constraint and to build up a relationship to other people based on equality. This is necessary in order to make cooperation work. In this new condition the child is able to be a master of his thoughts.

Defined by equality and mutual respect, the relations of cooperation . . ., constitute an equilibrated limit rather than a static system.

(Piaget, 1932, p. 402)

One must say that Piaget does not mean that in the cooperation condition the child has the opportunity to practice any pre-existent unconscious thought, although this is the case as we have seen before. It is rather the move into a free situation where the child is able to form equilibrated and adaptive knowledge about social relations in cooperation with his equals. The realization of this ideal equilibrium is impossible within an unequal social situation where adult constraint dominates (Fig 2).

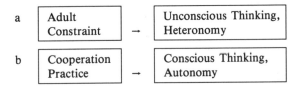

a | Adult Constraint | → | Unconscious Thinking, Heteronomy

b | Cooperation Practice | → | Conscious Thinking, Autonomy

Fig 2. The two phases of moral functioning according to Piaget.

Although Piaget gives us the impression that it is not the unconscious imported thinking that is practiced in order to become conscious, that is the case in his later work. In studying the formation of consciousness concerning reality, Piaget (1976, 1978, 1980) showed that the faulty description (unconscious but not imported thinking from the adults) by the child of his own action, becomes conscious in a process of contradiction between the faulty description of the action and the action itself. Thus, if there is always some unconscious thinking which guides adaptive action, then that cognitive function would be in a position to admit even imported unconscious adaptive thinking. That thinking could guide adaptive action in a social situation, with first disequilibrium and then consciousness as a result. It is reasonable then to regard Fig 2a and Fig 2b as connected to each other. That should mean that the move into an ideal equal social relationship to other people can even be combined with "adult constraint" as an instruction condition in order for the child to became a master of his social thought and action (Fig 3). It is reasonable also to hypothesize that this conscious-making process is taking place in a purely cognitive way, with no action involved, when the internalized thinking refers to moral stories and not to real social situations for the child.

But we may ask why such thinking given to a child by adult authority should be internalized by the child and acquire the same cognitive function as the child's own unconscious thinking which guides adaptive action.

First, it would be impossible to find any social relationship that is equal. Piaget (1932, p. 402) says that: ". . . the relations of constraint . . .

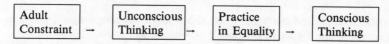

Fig 3. A conceptual model of Piaget's theory of moral development.

characterize most of the features of society as it exists . . ." Consequently, it is impossible to be liberated from constraint. It is present everywhere and operating on everyone. The way out of this is what the older Piaget clearly suggests: the practice of and the reflection on action, social action in this case. This is also related to the non-existence of distinct and general stages, for there are no ideal heteronomous and autonomous social relations to cause a different kind of thinking and action. The influence from other people is present everywhere and all the time, such as the practice of that moral influence, which in turn can result in consciousness and liberation from constraint. Of course, more or less equal cooperation with people is necessary, because that is what social knowledge (moral thinking) is about, i.e., social relations and the social action within them. It is there that the child gets the chance to test and eventually to improve his social knowledge.

The most important factor, however, for the acceptance of instruction is the children's innate tendency to submit to adult authority, to imitate them and to accept their values and principles. According to Piaget, constraint and unilateral respect characterize most features of the child's relationship to adult world. It is a spontaneous tendency on the part of the child that is impossible to avoid:

> . . . it is not possible completely to avoid giving the child commands that are incomprehensible to it. In such cases — which are almost the rule in the traditional form of education based on authority — the mere fact of accepting the command almost invariably provokes the appearance of moral realism.
>
> (Piaget, 1932, p. 174)

This tendency was so strong that Piaget was not able to avoid it even with his own children. Nevertheless, Piaget considers this fact to be annoying, and therefore its importance lies only on its removal. He is concerned about the disastrous effects traditional education has upon children's moral and intellectual development. Of course, we may share Piaget's concern, but we can not ignore children's universal tendency to submit to adult authority. The temptation to attempt to incorporate it into a theory of development is very strong.

How can one explain the openness of children to the adult world? An explanation is provided by psychoanalysis. All children have to be identified with their parents. The boy, in order to solve the Oedipal conflict, is identified with his father, whereas the girl has been identified with her mother earlier.

A result of this identification is the formation of the superego which becomes the conscience of the child. The superego takes over the moral role of the parents. Freud (1940/1976, p. 391) defines identification as "... the assimilation of one ego to another one, as a result of which the first ego behaves like the second in certain respects, imitates it and in a sense takes it up into itself."

Furthermore, there may be an evolutionary explanation to the openness of children to the adult world. Adults already live in the world where the child is going to live, so he is going to get a good chance to adapt to that world if he learns from the adult who is supposed to be adapted to it. It is a form of imitation, and this is an innate tendency present directly after birth (Kugiumutzakis, 1985). The function of this kind of imitation is for the child to obtain information and knowledge about his actions upon the world. The acceptance of adult constraint seems to be necessary, because man's action is not regulated strictly by instincts. He has to construct the knowledge, but he even has to learn from what is already constructed by other people in society.

> For the fundamental fact of human psychology is that society, instead of remaining almost inside the individual organism as in the case of animals prompted by their instincts, becomes cristallized almost entirely outside the individuals. In other words social rules . . . cannot be constituted, transmitted, or preserved by means of an internal biological heredity, but only through the external pressure exercised by individuals upon each other.
>
> (Piaget, 1932, p. 183)

In spite of that, Piaget does not incorporate this thesis into his theory. He recognizes explicitly the great impact of adult authority on the formation of autonomous thinking. Still, he does not attempt to investigate its eventual positive effects. He regards it as an impediment to development which has to be removed.

Consequently, he proposes that traditional education, which is based on authority, has to be replaced by democratic pedagogy which promotes cooperation.

> The adult must therefore be a collaborator and not a master, from this double point of view, moral and rational. But conversely, it would be unwise to rely upon biological "nature" alone to ensure the dual progress of conscience and intelligence, when we realize to what extent all moral as all logical norms are the result of cooperation.
>
> (Piaget, 1932, p. 412)

A collaborator is then needed. Still one may ask: how is it possible to purify his influence, and why is he needed? These questions raise some certain problems for the Piagetian theory. One can not at the same time consider that "constraint . . . strengthens egocentric features" (1932, p. 184) and that the child needs a "collaborator." Of course, a solution to this problem may be the introduction of the hypothesis that the "collaborator" is in fact instructing the child how to think and act by providing him with new knowledge. Leading the child into problem situations and creating disequilibrium for him, just as Socrates did in his dialogues, is not relying "upon biological 'nature' alone." To create a problem, to define it, and to organize it in order to solve it, is not a simple process. A lot of knowledge is necessary, which in this case is provided by the "collaborator" or the instructor. That knowledge is accepted by the child who uses it in his social action, and consequently he becomes conscious of that. The clear and organized presentation of the problem disequilibrates the equilibrated cognitive functions of the child who is then challenged to reestablish the equilibrium by reorganizing his thinking.

To summarize, Piaget was the first to offer a theory about the independence and conscious-making process of children's moral thinking. Although he regards external influence as strengthening the egocentric tendency of the child, he implicitly admits its value as an aid to development. Of course, this is not enough, and consequently he does not incorporate it as a positively active factor in his theory. The implication is not that authority does not impede development. Such is often the case, as Piaget has shown, but its influence on the acceleration of development towards independent and creative moral thinking remains to be investigated.

The sources of moral development

Unfortunately, Piaget's theory of the formation of autonomous moral thinking has not influenced the main stream of research in the area of moral development. In comparison with Kohlberg, we may conclude that Piaget's impact on moral theory is minimal. On the other hand, Piaget's original study is often referred to, but this reference is usually followed by some amount of misinterpretation, or at least a shift of focus away from the heteronomy-autonomy dimension. Furthermore, the role of instruction as a cause for the formation of subjective and autonomous moral thinking has not been investigated.

Nevertheless, Crowley (1968) attempted to study the effect of training on the acceleration of subjective thinking. He found that the two training conditions, (1) labeling the naughtier character in the story followed by a reward for subjective response and, (2) labeling plus discussion before the reward, produced a significant shift towards subjective reasoning. The same tendency was also observed in the two corresponding training conditions in which nonmoral stories were used, although the observed effect was not as clear as in the two former conditions. Crowley explained these results as dependent on the decentering from the objective features of the stories, provoked by the training conditions. However, the use of labeling together with discussion and reward in the same training conditions did not permit the discerning of the influence of instruction.

A very interesting investigation was conducted by Lickona (1971, 1976). In his doctoral dissertation he studied the influence of four different training conditions on the shift of objective moral thinking to subjective moral thinking. In that study objective children received different training in order to advance to the subjective phase of moral judgment.

The first training condition was decentering (DC). During the training phase Lickona told the children stories similar to those in the pretest, but in the training phase, when he told the stories, he showed pictures to the children. The hypothesis was that the pictorial representation and the simultaneous consideration of both intentions and consequences would have a combinative effect on the child's moral thinking. It is important to mention that no further instruction was given. The training condition was just that different form of presentation of the stories.

The second training condition was called peer-interaction (PI). That condition implied the simultaneous interviewing of an objective and a subjective child and the confrontation of their opposite judgments. It was hypothesized that the objective child would be motivated to shift to the higher phase. That shift was supposed to be caused by the cooperation and reciprocity which should take place between the children, and which should break down the objective child's egocentrism.

During the third training condition, adult-conflict (AC), the children were exposed to the contradictory moral judgments of two discussing adults. It was supposed that the contradictory messages should reduce adult constraint and create uncertainty. Thus the child should come into a situation of disequilibrium and start to reorganize his thoughts.

The fourth and most interesting condition was the didactic training (DI). During the training condition the experimenter presented the right answer to the child and explained why it was right. Although Lickona regarded this condition as contrary to Piaget's theory, he expected that any changes in that condition should diverge significantly from the other conditions.

Indeed, the results showed that the greatest change towards the subjective phase, both at training test and posttest, was motivated by the didactic training condition (Table 2).

Furthermore, the didactic training condition showed the greatest and the only significant generalization of gained subjective reasoning to stories with different content at Posttest. Those generalization stories were about

Table 2. Mean percentage of subjective responses for each experimental phase (Lickona, 1971).

	Pretest	Training test	Posttest
DC	11	33	43
PI	14	63	74
AC	24	63	53
DI	16	81	92

children's lies, whereas the training stories were only about motives versus consequences.

Lickona discussed these results, and he concluded that his study could not provide a definitive test of Piaget's hypotheses about the sources of shift in moral reasoning towards subjectivity. Lickona had hypothesized that the three first training conditions (DC, PI, AC) should motivate advancement to the subjective phase by causing disequilibrium in the cognitive processes of the objective children. Unfortunately, there were alternative interpretations of the obtained results.

The DC condition produced a relatively small increase in subjective reasoning. Moreover, that increase could be interpreted as a result of the concreteness of the medium (for which the child could use the higher form of thinking), rather as an effect of the Piagetian cognitive condition of decentering. That could be a matter of simple transformation of the subjective reasoning from the concrete to the abstract form of the stimulus material rather than a definitive reorganization of the child's thought.

The peer-interaction condition produced greater change, but the critical variable was not the confrontation per se, because the interaction between the children was limited since they were egocentric and adult directed. The obtained result could be interpreted as an effect of the exposition of the objective children to the subjective children's higher form of reasoning.

The same may be hypothesized even for the adult-conflict condition. The observed change could be caused by the presentation of the subjective reasoning rather than the context of two conflicting and contradictory adults.

That alternative explanation was strengthened much more by the significance of the results of the didactic-training condition. Indeed, at that condition the critical variable was the clearness, salience, and distinctiveness of the training stimulus, i.e., the instruction, which produced the greatest effect. Thus, according to the alternative interpretation, that clearness of the presentation of the higher form of reasoning at DI condition was the cause of the shift of the greatest number of children to subjective thinking. In that condition the alternative explanation was the most plausible one. Furthermore,

Lickona regarded the shift of reasoning at the DI condition as possibly a result of disequilibrium initiated by the instruction. That means that the instruction at DI condition could create a reorganization of the child's thought. Nevertheless, Lickona could not see how those results could be compatible with Piaget's theory.

As we have seen in our previous discussion, there are certain aspects of Piaget's theory that could allow the acceptance of the alternative explanation, i.e., that the clearness of the presentation of the higher reasoning causes the shift to the subjective phase of moral thinking. One aspect is that the Piagetian theory does indeed accept that there is always some unconscious thinking which guides the child's adaptive action. That is derived from the thesis of the time lag between thought and action. The other aspect is that the child's obedience to adult authority and the imitation function imply the internalization of unconscious thinking. Consequently, the internalized unconscious thinking could have an adaptive function if it were applied in a social context. That implementation could then, according to Piaget's disequilibration process, turn the unconscious thinking into conscious. Moreover, the Vygotskian critique of Piaget's theory provides the most important argument for a Piagetian explanation of Lickona's findings.

The paradox of instruction inducing moral development by using the unequal bond of child obedience to adult authority is not relevant in the case of motives vs. damage stories or concept of lying stories, since the issue here is only about intention. However, it could be relevant in stories about equality and authority such as in situations where the rules of a game would be at the focus of instruction or in real social situations where some power structure and unequal relations always exist among the individuals. Moreover, it is not easy to claim that the instruction does not initiate disequilibrium and consequently cause a reorganization of the thought. The results obtained at adult-conflict and peer-interaction conditions, as the results of other studies, revealed that the experimentally trained "downward" change was either insignificant or unstable and could not be generalized to other situations.

INSTRUCTION AND DEVELOPMENT

We have already seen that there are certain aspects of Piagetian theory that could allow instruction to play a positive role in the child's intellectual development, but any attempt to a definitive incorporation of instruction in the Piagetian theory was deemed to fail until Vygotsky's critique of Piaget became known. Vygotsky, in fact, complements the Piagetian theory by introducing the notion of influence of culture and the role of instruction. In regard to egocentrism, Piaget's thesis is that adult constraint strengthens it. The child is isolated, and he is unable to take the other's perspective. Then, the sense of reciprocity is not developed. Thus, we can not expect any intellectual development, nor the development of autonomous moral thinking when its ground, i.e., cooperation, does not exist.

Vygotsky overturned Piaget's arguments by asserting that the child is in fact socialized from the beginning. He uses adult speech in order to guide his action:

> Thus our schema of development — first social, then egocentric, then inner speech — contrasts both with the traditional behaviorist schema — vocal speech, whisper, inner speech — and with Piaget's sequence — from nonverbal autistic thought through egocentric thought and speech to socialized speech and logical thinking. In our conception, the true direction of the development of thinking is not from the individual to the socialized, but from the social to the individual.
>
> (Vygotsky, 1962, pp. 19—20)

Indeed, Piaget conceded that criticism: "I find myself in complete agreement with these hypotheses." (Piaget, 1962, p. 7).

Consequently, such a hypothesis must imply a different view of the relationship between learning and development. The Piagetian theory focuses its interest on the spontaneous development of the child. The initiative for development lies with the child and the role of the adult is restrained to that of a collaborator, i.e., to provide the necessary help that the child needs. Therefore, the research should be directed towards the study of spontaneous concepts and their development towards scientific ones. Vygotsky, on the other hand, maintains that instruction may play a decisive role for the development of scientific thinking.

> . . . the study of scientific concepts as such has important implications for education and instruction. Even though these concepts are not absorbed ready-made, in-

struction and learning play a leading role in their acquisition.

(Vygotsky, 1962, p. 86)

Thus, not only formal education or, in general, instruction by adults might have those effects, but even cooperation is considered to work in the same direction since the child is always exposed to instruction by his peers when he is interacting and cooperating with them (Vygotsky, 1978, p. 90). However, one can not avoid facing the question as to whether instruction in reality has any positive effect on development, when Piaget asserts that it may impede development, or if and why "nonspontaneous" concepts interact with "spontaneous."

Indeed, there is an obvious risk that the child does not accept at all, i.e., ignores totally, the knowledge given to him by instruction. Furthermore, it is possible that the child, despite the acceptance of the instruction, does not use it in his action, which may have the consequence that the imported knowledge remains stable and fixed as given by authority and in fact not learned. The strongest risk is that which Piaget points to: that knowledge, adopted through instruction given by an authority, may in fact guide action in a heteronomous way and strengthen adult constraint.

In order to avoid all those risks we have to take account of the interests of the children in studying the effect of instruction upon logico-mathematical and social development. The child is concerned only about what is relevant for him, consequently he guides his action only towards that. The equilibrium is disturbed only with regard to the child's adaptive efforts which express his interests. As we have even seen in our critique of Piaget, this does not mean that only the spontaneous acting and thinking leads to disequilibrium and development. Nevertheless, Piaget's theory is biased towards this thesis, but this has the advantage of eliminating the aforementioned risks.

Vygotsky, on the other hand, is more vulnerable to the accusation of being a proponent of traditional education.

> . . . what is transmitted by instruction is well assimilated by the child because it represents in fact an extension of some spontaneous constructions of his own. In such cases, his development is accelerated. But in other cases, the gifts of instruction are presented too soon or too late, or in a manner that precludes assimilation because it does not fit in with the child's spontaneous constructions. Then the child's development is impeded, or even deflected into bareness, as so often happens in the teaching of the exact sciences.
>
> (Piaget, 1962, p. 11)

As an attempt to provide an answer to that problem, Vygotsky (1978) introduced the hypothesis of the zone of proximal development. According to Vygotsky, instruction has to take into account the child's current function in order to influence the acceleration of development. In fact, the hypothesis of

51

the zone of proximal development is compatible with the Piagetian notion of assimilation for the intellectual development of the child. Furthermore, Vygotsky claimed that instruction not only accelerated development but that could promote development which would be impossible otherwise.

> . . . properly organized learning results in mental development and sets in motion a variety of developmental processes that would be impossible apart from learning. (Vygotsky, 1978, p. 90)

It is necessary to underline once more the fact that the theories of Vygotsky and Piaget are not incompatible or contradictory, but complementary to each other. Both Vygotsky and Piaget focused their interest on the issue of the liberation of man from any constraint, physical as well as social, by directing their research to the genesis of the higher intellectual functions. They sought to understand and explain the cognitive processes and the conditions that lead to the formation of that higher thinking. Vygotsky's contribution was that he completed the Piagetian theory by showing the significance of society and socially mediated knowledge for the development towards a higher and more adaptive intellectual functioning.

Unfortunately, those ideas of Vygotsky were not developed further in the research conducted later. Especially in the area of moral development the Piagetian-Vygotskian approach is totally neglected, and in the few attempts where Vygotsky is referred to, he is misunderstood. In some Soviet studies on moral development (Karpova & Petrushina, 1982/83; Subbotskii, 1981, 1983a, 1983b; Tudge, 1983; Yakobson & Pocherevina, 1983) the focus is centered on the transformation and generality of instructed principles, rather than on the thought processes themselves which guide the individual's adaptive efforts to social reality. That line of approach is, of course, alien to the main ideas of Vygotsky and Piaget, while it has more in common with learning theory, since it is not a study of the formation of autonomous thinking but the description of the conditions of the heteronomous moral function.

In conclusion we can say that Kohlberg's theory is not adequate for an explanation of all the aspects of the individual's moral function. Although it provides evidence for the movement of moral thinking towards abstract thinking, it considers morality as the following of certain principles, and development as the discovery — and not the construction — of them by the people who are going to use them. This theory is about the adaptation of the individual to a certain society's morality. It is not a theory of the formation of morality by the individuals living together in a society, and it does not describe the role of the psychological processes in doing that, such as the influence of prevalent morality upon them.

Piaget's theory answers most of the issues omitted by Kohlberg. This theory is not restricted only to the description of the predominating characteristics of moral function at different stages, but it focuses, too, on the process of development towards independent moral thinking and action. It is the moving out from a situation of adult constraint and into a situation of cooperation among equal individuals. That is understood as the ideal condition for the most adaptive moral function. Despite the enormous impact that authority values may have on moral development, Piaget regards it as something to be eliminated in order for development to occur, and, consequently, he does not attempt to study its influence on the formation of autonomous moral thinking in detail, or from a different perspective. Thus, Lickona could not give a Piagetian explanation to his results.

On the other hand, certain answers to the role of external influence on the development of moral thinking have been given by Kohlberg, Turiel and learning theory, but these, although they provide evidence for its positive role, are not compatible with the Piagetian theory's focus on the formation of independent thought.

Vygotsky is the researcher who showed the possibility of unifying instruction with the development of independent scientific thinking. Thus, given that there is no difference in principle between thinking about physical and social relations, we may assume that external influence may play a positive role in the formation of autonomous and adaptive moral thinking.

Instruction can be understood as an attempt by way of planned influence to enhance the functional level of social thinking and action by interrupting the individual's ongoing moral function which, of course, already has a certain adaptive value. The acceptance of the instruction by the individual may result in the formation of a cognitive representation, which, although unconscious, guides social action or moral decision. That is what Piaget calls the heteronomy condition. However, the practice of the unconscious thought forces the individual to become conscious about it through reflection caused by the relative inefficiency of the guided adaptive efforts. In turn, the conscious thought guides action and reasoning, and the result is again reflected upon.

That latter function constitutes the autonomy condition. According to Piaget, this condition in cooperation is the ideal production of social knowledge. But as we have seen, it might be possible to initiate this by suitable instruction.

PART TWO
THE EMPIRICAL STUDIES OF
MORAL JUDGMENT

INSTRUCTION AND THE ACCELERATION OF DEVELOPMENT

As we have seen in our previous discussion the research in the area of moral development has not been concerned with the issue of the formation of autonomous moral thinking. That issue, which was the hard core of Piaget's theory has been almost totally neglected by the later investigators. It has been very popular to focus on the description of the outcomes of the development and not on the forces and processes of the development itself. Such a typical approach is the very influential theory of Kohlberg. Consequently, it has been within the framework of this theory that the research on the processes of the development itself has taken place.

Turiel (1966, 1969, 1974, 1977; Turiel & Rothman, 1972; Rest, Turiel & Kohlberg, 1969) directed his research to the transitional process from a lower to a higher stage in the scale of Kohlberg, and not towards the role of instruction for the development of autonomous moral thinking and action. Kohlberg's (1984, 1985) research on moral education is also limited to the description of individual and community characteristics and stages of development. Neither were the learning researchers interested in autonomous thinking (Bandura and McDonald, 1963; Aronfreed, 1961, 1963). On the other hand, the research which is influenced by Piaget's interest in the formation of autonomous thinking, is very rare. Although Lickona (1971) obtained the tremendous impact of didactic training on the development of subjective thinking, he could not explain it in Piagetian terms.

The objectives of the study

The aim of the present study is to provide empirical support for the ideas that have been discussed before, i.e., the positive role that the Vygotskian instruction may play for the stimulation of the development of Piagetian autonomy. In particular, the objective of the study is first to construct a method of instruction based on the previous discussed integration of the theories of Piaget and Vygotsky. This instruction, when given to the children, is supposed to stimulate the development of their moral thinking. The second and main objective of this study is to test empirically the effect of this instruction in order to determine whether the children would accept it and develop to a higher phase of moral thinking. Third, the study will control the stability of such a change over time, and the generality of the effect to new conditions.

The dependent variables

In the present study the dependent variables are not the children's thoughts and actions about the rules of a game. If that were the case we could maintain, without any hesitation, that we are studying the heteronomy-autonomy dimension, since the most salient characteristic of the autonomous phase is the independent formation of rules through mutual agreement. The dependent variables of this study are limited to moral judgments. They are clearly not variables of moral action.

Two dependent variables are assessed in the present study. The first is children's judgments about problems of responsibility. The child can base his judgment about responsibility for an action either on the intentions of the character's act in pairs of stories, or on the extent of the material damage caused by the character's action. This is valid for the Clumsiness and Stealing cluster of stories, but responsibility is the dependent variable even for the Lying cluster, since the child can justify his answer either by reference to the intention of the story character or to the plausibility of the content of the lie. In both clusters of stories the children can give either a subjective, or an objective justification of their judgment.

The other dependent variable is the children's judgments about problems of justice. The child can either accept the statements of authority as fair, or take into account the principle of equality. Consequently, the child can give either an authority-based, or an equality-based justification for his judgment about problems of justice.

These two dependent variables, justifications of judgments about issues of responsibility and justice, are considered to be sufficient for the determination of the child's phase of moral thinking. The justification about responsibility is one of the most salient characteristics of the phase of moral thinking, and the equality justice, which the child acquires through cooperation, is one of the most important concepts, necessary for the development of the autonomous phase of moral thinking and action (Piaget, 1932). Since the present study is limited to the area of moral thinking, we are not going to name the two phases of moral development studied here as Heteronomous and

Autonomous, but Objective-Authoritarian (OA) and Subjective-Equalitarian (SE), denoting the lower and the higher phases of moral thinking.

Rationales for the experimental procedures

There are four experimental phases in the present study: Pretest, Instruction phase, Training test, and Posttest three weeks later.

1. The Pretest is given in order to remove from the study the subjects that are proved to belong to the SE phase of moral thinking. Only the OA subjects are allowed to go on, so the Instruction can show its effect. The other function of the Pretest is to establish a base for the evaluation of this effect.

2. During the Instruction phase the experimenter simply tells the child the right answer and explains why it is right. It is clear that the effect of the Instruction on the acceleration of the development of moral thinking is not supposed to be caused by the mediation of any experience, i.e., a confrontation with reality, as it is the common understanding of Piagetian development. Rather, the effect of the Instruction is theoretically based on Vygotsky's theory of the zone of proximal development. That means that the Instruction causes its effect solely through the mediation of cognitive processes and only at a cognitive level.

It is supposed that by the presentation of the correct judgment and its rationale, some disequilibrium is created in the child's cognitive function. Then, equilibrium is obtained through the acceptance of the higher form of moral thinking. The child accepts the Instruction for he must have some unconscious experience of the contradictoriness of the lower form of moral thinking to reality. The Instruction makes him conscious about this contradictoriness, so the higher form gives him a chance to remove the contradiction and to establish a new balance. The further development is supposed to depend on the practice of the internalized thinking and the reflection upon it.

If we should accept the usual interpretation of Piaget, it would be contradictory to claim that such an Instruction stimulates development. Rather, it would be more appropriate to maintain that the Instruction should reinforce the child's moral realism and constraint as a result of the authoritarian role which is supposed to be played by the experimenter.

3. The role of the Training test, which is given immediately after the Instruction, is to assess the effect of the Instruction. The generality of the effect is controlled by using story items with different content than those which are explained at the Instruction phase.

4. The Posttest is given three weeks later in order to control the stability of

the effect of the Instruction, and to test its generality by using new and old stories.

5. The Control group is necessary for a comparison of the natural development of moral thinking to that which is manipulated experimentally through the Instruction.

Hypotheses

The hypotheses tested in the present study are:

1. The Instruction will produce a shift towards SE moral thinking at Training test, in judging about stories contrasting intentions to material damage, intentions to content of lies, and authority to equality.

2. This advancement to SE moral thinking will not be lost at the Posttest, three weeks later.

3. The acquired SE thinking will be generalized to stories with new content at Training test and Posttest.

Method

Subjects

The subjects in this study came from three public schools located in Athens. The sample was randomly selected out of that group of children whose ages ranged from 6 years and 7 months to 7 years and 6 months. The study was limited to this age-group for it is supposed that a majority of OA children are included there, while at the same time they are very close to a shift to the SE phase of moral thinking (Piaget, 1932).

Of all the 1st and 2nd grade children that were randomly selected only 10 proved to be SE thinkers at Pretest, so they were dismissed from the study. Hence, 107 children participated. They were 59 boys and 48 girls with a mean age of 7 years and 1 month for both groups.

The subjects were not tested by any intelligence test, and the success or failure of their school attendance was not taken into account.

Experimenter

The author of the present study served as the tester and instructor through all the experimental phases. The semi-structured interview, the standard instruction, the tape-recording of the interviews, the standard criteria for scoring, and the codification of the data by two naive judges were adopted in order to avoid any biases by the experimenter.

Pilot study

A pilot study was conducted before the main study. 10 randomly chosen children from one school participated. The aim of the pilot study was to select the most suitable Piagetian stories, the development of accurate instructions, and the shaping of the codification criteria.

It was shown that children confused different stories with similar content although they had a different theme, e.g., children confused a story of the Clumsiness-Stealing group in which a pair of scissors was involved with a story from the Lying group in which a pair of scissors was lost. Also, it seemed that some groups of stories were more difficult for children to understand. Considering that only a restricted number of story clusters and stories from each cluster could be adopted, those were selected which were easier to understand and which were not confused too often. It was also necessary to check how the Instruction functioned in an experimental situation, but no serious problems were observed.

Moral stories

Nine story items served in the study. These were the original Piagetian stories (Appendix A) translated to Greek. Each story item was presented in two forms at the same time: each story was told and presented pictorially to the subject (Appendix C). The pictorial presentation of the stories was selected in order to make them more vivid to the children. Yannopoulos-Mitsacos' (1984) Greek translation and the corresponding pictures were used.

These nine story items were divided into three clusters, consisting of three stories each, according to three different themes. Each of the three themes (intention vs. material consequences, intention vs. no intention, and equality vs. authority) was expressed in three story items, i.e., a total of nine story items.

1. Clumsiness and Stealing

Three pair of stories from the Clumsiness and Stealing (CS) cluster were adopted. At each experimental phase one story item was used. The theme of these stories was intention vs. material damage, i.e., good intention with great negative consequences in the one of the stories contrasting with bad intention and small negative consequences in the other story. The subjects could base the justification of their answers either on the good or bad intention of the story character (when they were judged to be SE thinkers), or on the extent of the material damage which was caused by the character's behavior in the other story (when they scored as OA thinkers).

2. Lying

The three pair of stories of the Lying (L) group were used in order to contrast the degree of falsity of a lie to its aim. These stories were not about the consequences of a lie, but they were about two story characters who did or did not have the intention of deliberately deceiving somebody in order to win something. Hence, intention was not contrasted with material damage, but with the lack of intention or the plausibility of the lie.

3. Equality and Authority

These three stories of Equality and Authority (EA) group were employed in the study in order to test if the judgments of the children about what was fair were more influenced by authority or by the concept of equality. The theme of these stories was about an adult allocating work duties among children, but in an unfair way. The subjects were asked to judge the fairness or unfairness of the act of the adult, and to comment on the acceptance or rejection of the duty by child character in the story. When the subjects showed respect for the authority of the adult character, they scored as OA thinkers, and when they defended equality, they scored as SE thinkers.

Item reliability

The problem was to be able to define the subject's phase of moral thinking at each test by using a satisfactory number of the most understandable story items from each cluster. The kind of story items is also important, but the clusters which were employed are satisfactory for the scoring of the moral phase (see the previous discussion about the dependent variables).

The number of the story items could not exceed three at each test, for it would be too arduous for the subject during the first session of the experiment which contained two tests and the Instruction phase (Fig 4).

Nevertheless, the number of three story items proved to be satisfactory for the definition of the subject's phase of moral thinking. These story items, one from each cluster, had to define the same moral phase at each test, or approximately the same, in order to ascertain if the present method was reliable.

Indeed, the results showed that the agreement on the phase of moral thinking among the story items in the Experimental group varied from 72.7% to 79.2% (Table 3).

Previous research employed more than three story items for the definition of the moral phase (Lickona, 1971; Yannopoulos-Mitsacos, 1984). Unfortunately, the homogeneity of the items was not reported. On the other hand, Kohlberg's Standard Issue Scoring showed a very high reliability which ranged from 0.92 to 0.96 for each interview form (Colby et al., 1983), whereas Rest's (1979) Defining Issues Test showed internal consistency reliability which ranged from 0.77 to 0.79. However, these elaborated instruments use items different from the Piagetian ones, and they operate in a different theoretical framework.

The selection of the story items from each cluster in the present study was made on the basis of the ease of comprehension by the subjects, and distinctiveness of the content from other story items employed in the test in order to avoid confusion.

Table 3. Percentage agreement of each cluster of items to moral phase at each test, and overall agreement at each test and experimental group.

	Pretest	Training test	Posttest	All
Exp.Gr.				
. CS	89.6	89.6	92.2	
L	92.2	94.8	90.9	
EA	90.9	94.8	94.8	
All	72.7	79.2	77.9	76.2
Contr.				
CS	90	—	86.7	
L	93.3	—	86.7	
EA	96.7	—	93.3	
All	80	—	66.7	73.3

Instructions before the tests

At the beginning of each experimental test phase the following instructions were given to the subject:

> I am going to show you some pictures and tell you three stories about some children who did different things. Listen carefully to them because we are going to talk about them when I am finished. Here comes the first story. . .

After the presentation of each story item the subject had to repeat it without looking at the corresponding picture, so the experimenter had the opportunity to control if he had understood the item and remembered it, by asking the subject:

"Would you like to tell me the stories/story I just told to you?"

During the repetition phase the experimenter helped the subject to correct his misunderstandings, and, if it was necessary, the experimenter told the stories once more. If he continued to be unable to understand them after the second telling, he was dismissed from the study. Only three subjects, two girls and one boy, did not understand the stories.

Immediately after the repetition followed the interview corresponding to each story item (Appendix B). The interviews were constructed so as to highlight the motivations behind the answers of the subjects, and to control the stability of their answers by asking several slightly different questions.

Procedure

Figure 4 represents a summary of the overall experimental design.

	Pretest	Instruction	Training test	Posttest
Exp.Gr. N = 77	3 items/ Subject	Yes	3 new items/S	3 new & Pre items/S
Control N = 30	3 items/ Subject	No	No	3 new items/S

Fig 4. A summary of the experimental design.

The experiment was conducted in two different sessions. The Pretest, Instruction, and Training test were given on the same occasion to each individual subject. The Posttest was given three weeks later. The story items which were adopted in the study were counterbalanced. Then, a corresponding number to N and experimental tests from all possible combinations of the items and their order of presentation were randomly selected. All tests and the Instruction were administered individually in a separate room of the school.

1. Pretest

The pretest had two functions. The first was to select the OA Ss among the children who had been chosen at random to the experiment from their age group (6y,7m to 7y,6m). Only 10 children proved to be SE thinkers, i.e., they had been judged as SE's on at least two of the three story items at Pretest. These children were dropped from the study. The rest of them, 107 children who were scored as OA thinkers, were randomly distributed to the Experimental and Control groups and continued through the whole experiment.

The other function of the Pretest was to serve as a basis for comparison to each S's scoring at the following tests. Three story items, one from each cluster, were used for the scoring of the S's phase of moral thinking at each test.

2. Instruction

After the Pretest, which was the first evaluation of the S's moral phase, followed the Instruction phase of the experiment. The subject received the Instruction by the experimenter. The aim was to guide the moral thinking and judgment of the subject towards the SE phase.

First, the experimenter asked the subject to repeat the Pretest stories and his judgments and justifications about them, in order to control if the subject could retrieve them from his memory:

> Do you remember the stories I told you? Tell them! Do you remember who you said was the naughtiest child? Why?
> or
> Do you remember if the request of the parent was fair, and what should the child do?

After the subject had retrieved the stories and his judgments about them, the experimenter presented the SE versions about the same stories to the subject by telling him:

> I think that the naughtier child is. . .(character's name) because. . .
> (about the CS items)
> . . .the worst thing we can do (damage or stealing), is that we do with bad inten-

tions, which means that we do not mean well. We do it in order to win something for ourselves just as . . .(character's name) did, because he/she wanted to . . .(character's bad intention). On the other hand, it is not as bad if we meant well when we do something (damage or stealing), which means that we had a good intention when we did it as . . .(the good character's name) did, because he/she wanted to . . .(his/her good intention).

(about the L items)
. . . a bad lie is one that we tell to somebody when we want to cheat him in order to win something or to avoid something unpleasant. That means that we have bad intentions. So . . .(the bad character) is the naughtier child. But . . .(the good character) did not tell a real lie because he did not mean to cheat anybody. He did not have any bad intentions. So, if we tell something that is not the truth, and we do not mean to cheat anybody, it is not a bad lie.

The experimenter told to the Ss about the EA items:

It was not fair asking the girl/boy to do all the work alone. The parents have to allocate the work equally among their children, and, if they do not do so, they are not fair. What the parents say is not always fair. It depends on what they say and how they treat their children. When the parent asks his/her child to do something that is unfair, the child need not obey him/her. The child may do what the parent asks, but not because he/she is afraid to be punished. Rather, he/she does this because he/she loves his/her parent and wants to help him/her in spite of his/her unfairness.

When the presentation of the SE versions was finished the experimenter asked the subjects to repeat them by using the following questions:

Did you understand what I told you?
Tell me who was the naughtier child in the story . . .(CS)?Why? Who would you punish more? Why? When is a child naughty, and when is he not naughty?
In the other story . . .(L), who told the worst lie? Why? Who would you punish more if you were his parent and knew the truth? Why? When does a child tell a bad lie, and when does he not?
In the last story . . .(EA), was the request of the parent fair? Why? What should the child do? Why? Are the parents always fair? When should the children obey their parents? Why?

During this last phase the experimenter corrected the subject if he showed that he had misunderstood the instructions.

The instructions were focused explicitly on the concepts of intention and equality, since a simple explanation of the higher form of moral thinking was not supposed to start a shift towards the SE moral phase. These concepts expressed and codified concrete rules about that form of higher thinking. The meaning of the above instructions was to guide the subject to SE moral thinking through the learning of more abstract concepts, like intention and equality, i.e., rules that could be applied to all the stories of a cluster. So, it was assumed possible for the subjects to transform their learned capacity of SE moral thinking to other situations, i.e., to new story items in the following tests.

3. Training test

Immediately after the Instruction the Ss received the Training test. Three new story items were used, one from each group of stories. The effect of the Instruction and its generality to new stories were assessed at this test.

4. Posttest

Three weeks later a Posttest was given in order to assess the stability of the effect and its generality by using new and the Pretest story items. The estimation of the generality of the effect was done by the comparison of the scores on the new items with the scores on the Pretest stories. Another function of this test was to show the spontaneous developmental tendency of moral thinking after the acceptance or lack of acceptance of the Instruction by the Ss.

Evaluation and codification

The evaluation of the tape-recorded answers to the interview questions was done by the experimenter and two independent judges. The subject's answer to each story item was scored either SE or OA. In addition, a further evaluation, of the phase of moral thinking at each experimental phase, was done. That evaluation was based on the subject's scoring on each of the three story items at each experimental phase, so that the majority of the SE or the OA responses determined the moral phase of the subject. That means that, when all three responses were evaluated, SE or OA, the subject was scored according to the corresponding moral phase. When only two of the responses were evaluated as being at the same phase, that determined the subject's moral phase at each test.

The evaluation of the answers was dependent on the motivations or the justifications that the subjects were asked to give, rather than on the correctness of the answer itself. The identification of the subject with the "good" character in the story item was not regarded sufficient. On the contrary, during the interview which followed the story telling, the subjects had to explain why they preferred to sympathize with the "good" character.

The evaluation of the subject's answers was based on the following criteria:

1. The subject was scored OA when:

- The subject based his judgment either on the extent of the material damage caused by the "good" character's action in the story, or on the limited material damage caused by the "bad" character's action, and not on the intentions behind the actions. The case was the same if the subject regarded the material damage caused by the "bad" character's action as very serious but he actually failed to discern the "bad" intention.

- The subjects, in trying to explain their judgments, focused only on the content of the lie and not on the "bad" or "good" intention of telling the lie. By content was meant the plausibility of the "ill"-intentioned character's lie or the implausibility of the "good" character's lie.

- The subject recognized the request of the authority as fair, or was ambivalent to the fairness or unfairness of the request, but he always accepted obedience to it.

2. The subject was scored SE when:

- The subject discerned the "good" intention or the absence of "bad" intention behind the action of the "good" character, or if he referred to the "bad" intention or the absence of "good" intention behind the action of the "bad" character.

- The subject focused his justification on the intention of the liar, rather on the content of the lie.

- The subject recognized what was fair or unfair, and did not accept obedience to authority or did it but with sufficient explanation (see the Instruction about the EA items).

Those criteria were focused on the subject's motivations of his answers. Sometimes it happened that a subject vacillated between an OA and SE justification. In that case he was scored as OA.

When the subject started with an OA response and ended up with a SE one, or vice-versa, he was scored according to his second response if he persisted in that.

Interrater reliability

The evaluation of the subject's answers was done by the experimenter (E) and two judges (A and B). The agreement among them varied from 89.2% to 97.3% in judging the S's moral phase for each cluster of items separately, and from 86.5% to 97.6% in the phase for all the clusters at each test. The Phi correlation coefficient (Guilford, 1956) varied from 0.73 to 0.95 (Table 4).

Table 4. Percentage interrater agreement and Phi correlation.

	CS	L	EA	Moral phase
EA				
Agreement	91.9%	89.2%	89.2%	86.5%
Phi	0.83	0.79	0.79	0.73
EB				
Agreement	91.9%	97.3%	94.6%	89.2%
Phi	0.83	0.95	0.89	0.78
AB				
Agreement	94.6%	91.9%	95.6%	97.6%
Phi	0.88	0.84	0.89	0.94

Previous research in the area of moral development showed a variation of interjudge agreement from 0.48 to 0.98 (Snarey, 1985). Yannopoulos-Mitsacos reported a correlation between three judges which varied from 0.60 to 0.92.

Validity

The problem of validity can not be answered through correlation to any external criterion. It seems to be very difficult to find such criteria. Besides, any correlation to the results of most of the previous research can not be accepted since it has a different theoretical basis, apart from Lickona's (1971) study which showed similar results (Tables 2 & 5).

The above reported scores on the homogeneity of the test device and the interrater agreement were accepted as a measure of validity. This is, of course, a construct validity since the homogeneity of the evaluations of the phases of moral thinking, like the high interrater agreement, point only to the quality of the method. The accuracy of the method in determining the phases of moral thinking may be seen as a measure of the "reality" of these phases and of the expected effect of the Instruction on the shift from the lower phase to the higher one.

Results

During the Pretest 10 subjects proved to be SE thinkers, so they were dismissed from the study. The rest, 107 subjects, received the Instruction and the following tests. The analysis of the results focused on the effect of the Instruction, on the following spontaneous developmental tendencies, and on the impact of sex and age. The analysis of the Posttest results was based on the new story items. The function of the Pretest stories at Posttest was to compare the scores on them with the scores on the new items as an indication of the generality of the effect.

Instruction

The results revealed that the Instruction had a very high effect on the acceleration of the development of moral thinking from the OA to the SE phase. 66 (85.7%) subjects of the Experimental group advanced to the SE phase and remained there at the Posttest, whereas only 5 Controls (16.7%) developed to the next phase during the same time period (Table 5). This difference was highly significant both at Training test ($x^2 = 67.07$, df = 1, p < 0.001) and at the Posttest ($x^2 = 46.05$, df = 1, p < 0.001) (Guilford, 1956).

The separate analysis of each cluster of story items showed similar results. The Instruction's effect varied from 77.9% to 88.3% (Table 6). Three x^2 tests showed that these results were highly significant (Table 7).

The old Pretest story items were presented again at Posttest, after the completion of the interview with the new stories. These Pretest stories were used during the Instruction. The experimenter had presented and explained the right answers to them and the subjects had repeated them. A comparison of the SE and OA responses on the Pretest stories with the responses on the new stories showed that there was a mean of 98.7% SE responses when the subjects judged the Pretest stories in contrast to the 85.7% of the new stories (Table 8). This difference was significant: $x^2 = 9.038$, df = 1, p < 0.01.

Table 5. Number (in parenthesis) and percentage of SE Ss at each test for all clusters of items.

	Pretest	Training test	Posttest
Experimental Group N = 77	0	85.7% (66)	85.7% (66)
Control Group N = 30	0	— —	16.7% (5)

Table 6. Number and percentage of SE Ss at each test for for each cluster of story items.

	Pretest	Training test	Posttest
CS			
Exper.	10.4% (8)	77.9% (60)	80.5% (62)
Contr.	10.0% (3)	—	23.3% (7)
L			
Exper.	7.8% (6)	80.5% (62)	79.2% (61)
Contr.	6.7% (2)	—	16.7% (5)
EA			
Exper.	9.1% (7)	88.3% (68)	85.7% (66)
Contr.	3.3% (1)	—	10.0% (3)

Table 7. The results of the x^2 test of the effect of the Instruction at Training and Posttest.

	Training test	Posttest
CS:	$x^2 = 42.12$ df = 1 p < 0.001	$x^2 = 30.85$ df = 1 p < 0.001
L:	$x^2 = 48.96$ df = 1 p < 0.001	$x^2 = 35.72$ df = 1 p < 0.001
EA:	$x^2 = 68.11$ df = 1 p < 0.001	$x^2 = 54.07$ df = 1 p < 0.001

Table 8. Percentage (nr of Ss in parenthesis) of the OA and SE judgments on the Pretest and New items at Posttest, Experimental Group.

	OA	SE
Pretest items:	1.3% (1)	98.7% (76)
New items:	14.3% (11)	85.7% (66)

The spontaneous developmental tendencies

Another interesting aspect of the results is the tendency of the shifts between SE and OA during the time period from Training test to Posttest. 36.4% of the OA thinking subjects at Training test moved to the SE phase at Posttest, whereas only 7.6% of SE thinkers became OA's at Posttest. That difference was significant: $x^2 = 5.089$, $df = 1$, $p < 0.02$. The same tendency was observed for each cluster of stories separately (Table 9). CS: $x^2 = 8.392$, $df = 1$, $p < 0.01$; L: $x^2 = 5.089$, $df = 1$, $p < 0.02$; EA: $x^2 = 8.578$, $df = 1$, $p < 0.01$. That showed clearly that the advancement to the SE phase of moral thinking was stable.

Table 9. Percentage and number (in parenthesis) of change from SE to OA phase of moral thinking for all clusters and for each each in experimental group.

	Training test		Posttest
All clusters	SE: 85.7% (66)	→	OA: 7.6% (5)
of items:	OA: 14.3% (11)	→	SE: 36.4% (4)
CS:	SE: 77.9% (60)	→	OA: 15.0% (9)
	OA: 22.1% (17)	→	SE: 64.7% (11)
L:	SE: 80.5% (62)	→	OA: 13.3% (8)
	OA: 19.5% (15)	→	SE: 46.7% (7)
EA:	SE: 88.3% (68)	→	OA: 8.8% (6)
	OA: 11.7% (9)	→	SE: 55.6% (5)

The comparison of the spontaneous developmental tendencies of the moral thinking of the Ss in the Experimental Group, after the presentation of the Instruction, with the spontaneous developmental tendencies of the Controls showed that there was a nonsignificant difference between them ($x^2 = 1.09$, $df = 1$, $p < 0.3$). The Experimental Ss showed a tendency to shift to the SE phase during the time between the Training test and the Posttest, whereas the Controls showed a weaker tendency to do so (Table 10). The mean age for the Experimental Ss was 7y, 5.5m and for the Controls 7y, 2m. Both were older than the mean age in their whole groups (Table 12).

Table 10. Percentage (number of Ss in parenthesis) of the difference in the developmental tendency from OA at Pre and Training tests to SE at Posttest between the Experimental and the Control groups.

	OA (Pre & Training)	SE (Posttest)
Experim. Gr. N = 77	100% (11)	36.4% (4)
Control Gr. N = 30	100% (30)	16.7% (5)

Sex

Although boys tended to return to OA thinking between the Training test and the Posttest and the girls tended to advance to the SE phase more than the boys, the statistical analysis did not reveal any significant difference between the two groups with regard to the effect of the Instruction. The results showed the SE boys decreased from the 88.4% of the sample at Training test to 83.7% at Posttest, whereas the SE girls increased from 82.4% to 88.2% (Table 11). A x^2 test showed that the difference was not significant: $x^2 = 0.122$, $df = 2$, $p < 0.9$. Similar results were obtained in the analysis of each cluster of story items:

CS: $x^2 = 0.404$, $df = 2$, $p < 0.9$;
L: $x^2 = 0.6125$, $df = 2$, $p < 0.8$;
EA: $x^2 = 0.034$, $df = 2$, $p < 0.99$.

Table 11. Percentage and number (in parenthesis) of SE Ss at the tests and all clusters of items, each cluster, and sex.

	Pretest	Training test	Posttest
All:			
M(43)	0	88.4% (38)	83.7% (36)
F(34)	0	82.4% (28)	88.2% (30)
CS:			
M(43)	11.6% (5)	83.7% (36)	79.1% (34)
F(34)	8.8% (3)	70.6% (24)	82.4% (28)
L:			
M(43)	9.3% (4)	86.0% (37)	76.7% (33)
F(34)	5.9% (2)	73.5% (25)	82.4% (28)
EA:			
M(43)	9.3% (4)	88.4% (38)	83.7% (36)
F(34)	8.8% (3)	88.2% (30)	88.2% (30)

Age

The older subjects proved to be more resistant to the Instruction than the younger ones both at Training test and at Posttest. The mean age for the SE thinking subjects was 7 years and 1 month when the age of the OA thinkers was 7 years and 4 months at Training test and 7 years and 3 months at Posttest (Table 12). Two Mann-Whitney U tests (Mendenhall, McClave & Ramey, 1977) showed that these differences were significant: at Training test: $U = 537.5$, $p < 0.0055$; at Posttest: $U = 512$, $p < 0.015$. On the other hand the

Controls showed the opposite tendency. The older subjects (7 years, 2 months) shifted to the SE phase, whereas the younger ones (7 years, 1 month) remained at the OA phase. But that difference was not significant: $U = 79$, $p < 0.18$.

Table 12. Mean age for SE and OA judgments (nr of Ss in parenthesis) at each test for the Experimental and the Control groups.

	Pretest	Training test	Posttest
Exp.			
SE:	—	7y, 1m (66)	7y, 1m (66)
OA:	7y, 1m (77)	7y, 4m (11)	7y, 3m (11)
Con.			
SE:	—	—	7y, 2m (5)
OA:	7y, 1m	—	7y, 1m (25)

DISCUSSION

The main hypothesis of the present study, that the Instruction would produce a shift towards SE moral thinking, has been confirmed by the results. The Instruction stimulated the development of the moral judgment of approximately 86 percent of the lower-thinking subjects to the higher phase. This effect was not only high, but it was also possible to generalize to new story items at the posttests. These stories were different from the Pretest stories which the Instruction explained.

The results of the present study proved to be resistant to time. During the three week period between the Training test and the Posttest the effect remained at the same high level. The spontaneous upward movement of the Subjects who did not internalize the Instruction was significantly higher from the downward movement of the SE Subjects. That finding supports furthermore the stability of the Instruction effect. Moreover, there was a nonsignificant difference in the spontaneous developmental tendencies towards the SE phase between the Experimental and the Control Group. Nevertheless, this difference is very interesting for the assumption that the children who did not shift to the higher phase in spite of the presentation of the Instruction may be more prone to develop later than children who had not been instructed, like the Controls. On the other hand, this small difference may be dependent on the age difference between the Experimentals and the Controls, although these subjects were the older ones in each group. Since the difference was not significant, no further analysis was done.

In addition, the gained advancement to the higher phase of moral thinking was present even if new story items were used at Training test and Posttest. At these tests the effect was generalized to 85.7% of the new story items while the transformation of the effect over time to the old Instruction stories, at Posttest, was a little higher, 98.7%. We can not say that there was not any generality in spite of the significance of the difference. First, the observed shift to the SE phase was the same both at Training test and at Posttest. And second, the transformation of the SE ability over time to the old Pretest stories at Posttest may be seen as a matter of memory and not as a deeper reorganization of the cognitive functions.

No significant difference was observed between the sexes. The Instruction had the same effect on both the girls and the boys.

The high effect of the Instruction, its stability and generality confirms the hypothesis about its ability to stimulate the development of moral judgment. Theoretically, the above results, which were obtained through the use of a reliable method, are in accordance with the previous discussion about the application of the Vygotskian notion on the positive role of instructions for the stimulation of the development of logico-mathematical thinking to the area of moral thinking.

On the other hand, the age results showed that the younger subjects, instead of the older, as one could normally expect, were more prone to internalize the Instruction. The younger subjects showed a higher rate of SE responses, whereas the older ones were more resistant to the Instruction. Obviously, the older subjects did not accept the Instruction with the same eagerness as the younger did. Although the age difference was not greater than two or three months a possible explanation is that the older subjects were not as easily influenced by the authority of the experimenter. It was supposed that the Instruction when internalized would initiate the disequilibration—equilibration cognitive processes. Then, if the subject would not accept the Instruction, because he had been emancipated from the opinions of an authority like the authority of the concrete instructor, the above process would not be initiated and the result would be no development. Of course, this does not mean that the theory of the zone of proximal development is not valid (Vygotsky, 1978). We may maintain that the Instruction (its form and content) and the authority of the Instructor of the present study did not correspond to the developmental level of the older subjects. It is supposed that another kind of instruction given by a different authority should stimulate the development of the older subjects' moral thinking, such as the Instructor and the Instruction of the present study did for the younger ones.

INSTRUCTOR AND DEVELOPMENT

The main idea tested in the previous study was that instruction can accelerate the development of moral judgment. This hypothesis had its origin in the Piagetian-Vygotskian theory. Thus, the items used in that study were the original Piagetian stories. As discussed earlier, this theory focuses on the heteronomy-autonomy dimension of moral development, i.e., the liberation from adult constraint, especially the EA items.

But, that immediately raises the issue of the role of the instructor. Is the instructor really mediating some adaptive thinking, or is the child being simply influenced by the instructor's/tester's authority to judge according to his ideas? Was the high effect of instruction dependent on its cognitive value, or was it the result of the experimenter's authority? These questions became more significant when it was shown that the older children did not internalize the instructions (Table 12). A possible explanation of that result could be that these children did not accept the authority of the instructor, and, since one could suppose that they were more liberated from adult constraint, they retained their own OA judgments. That means that the authority of the instructor could have played some role during the following testing.

As an attempt to answer these questions about the role of the instructor on the effect of the instruction, a new study was designed. In the experimental phase of this study the instructor and the tester were different persons, while the same person served as both instructor and tester at control phase. It was supposed that this variation could allow us to test whether the high effect of the instruction was simply the result of the instructor's authority, since he was the tester of this effect.

Thus, the objective of this study was to test the effect of the instructor's personal authority on the internalization of the instruction and its influence on the acceleration of moral judgment. The same experimental design as in the previous study was used as well as the same dependent variables, i.e., justifications of judgments about issues of responsibility and justice.

The hypotheses tested in the present study were:

1. The instruction will promote a similar high acceleration of the development of moral judgment as in the previous study.

2. There will not be any significant difference between the experimental phase where the instructor and the tester are different persons, and in the control phase where they are identical.

Method

Subjects

The subjects were 31 Greek-speaking pre-school and school children (15 boys and 16 girls) from the Greek-speaking day-care centers and elementary schools of Stockholm and Uppsala, Sweden. Their age ranged from 5y,8m to 6y,10m with a mean of 6y,3m. From the randomly selected group of 35 children, only 4 proved to be SE thinkers at Pretest, so they were excluded from the study. The subjects understood and spoke the Greek language on a satisfactory level.

Experimenters

In the experimental phase the author served as the tester and a psychology student served as the instructor. In the control phase the author served both as tester and instructor.

Design

A similar design as in the previous study (Fig 4) was adopted. In the experimental phase the tester and the instructor were different persons, but in the control phase, in which instruction and training test were also given, these two roles were played by the same person (Fig 5).

	Pretest	Instruction	Training test	Posttest
Exp.Gr. N = 15	3 items/ Subject	by the Instructor	3 new items/S	3 new items/S
Control N = 16	3 items/ Subject	by the Tester	3 new items/S	3 new items/S

Fig 5. A summary of the experimental design

In the present study the Pretest items were not tested again at Posttest. The Posttest was given three weeks later than the Pretest and Training test, which were given on the same occasion.

The procedure was the same as in the previous study, except for the variation of the instructor's and tester's roles. The tests were given in the same way. Also, the same Instruction was used, as well as the same criteria for the evaluation of the subjects' judgments.

Reliability

The agreement of each cluster of items to the evaluated phase of moral thinking at each test varied from 80% to 100%. The total agreement among the clusters of items at each test varied from 66.7% to 81.3%. The all-test agreement of the experimental group was 71.1% and of the control group was 79.2% (Table 13). The overall agreement of the item clusters in the whole study was 75.3%.

Two judges evaluated the judgments of the subjects. The agreement between them on each subject's moral phase was 88.5%, and their agreement for each group of items varied from 88.5% to 92.3%. The Phi correlation coefficient (Guilford, 1956) varied from 0.72 to 0.78 (Table 14).

Table 13. Percentage agreement of each cluster of items to moral phase at each test, and overall agreement at each test and group.

	Pretest	Training test	Posttest	All
Exp.Gr.				
CS	100	80	93.3	
L	93.3	93.3	86.7	
EA	80	100	86.7	
All	73.3	73.3	66.7	71.1
Contr.				
CS	87.5	93.8	93.8	
L	93.8	93.8	87.5	
EA	100	87.5	100	
All	81.3	75	81.3	79.2

Table 14. Percentage interrater agreement and Phi correlation.

	CS	L	EA	Moral phase
Agreement	83.5%	92.3%	88.5%	88.5%
Phi	0.74	0.78	0.72	0.72

Results

The results showed clearly that the effect of the instruction was very high. Thus, 73.3% of the experimental subjects and 75% of the controls moved to the SE phase at Training test. At Posttest 80% of the experimentals and 87.5% of the controls were found to be at the SE phase (Table 15). Although the controls showed a slightly higher developmental tendency a x^2 test (Guilford, 1956) revealed that the difference was not significant: $x^2 = 0.013$, $df = 1$, $p < 0.95$.

Table 15. Percentage (nr in parenthesis) of SE judgments at each test for all clusters of stories.

	Pretest	Training test	Posttest
Exper. Gr. N = 15	0	73.3% (11)	80.0% (12)
Control Gr. N = 16	0	75.0% (12)	87.5% (14)

The same high effect of instruction was observed for each cluster of stories separately (Table 16), and the difference between the experimental and the control groups was not significant for any of these story clusters.
CS: $x^2 = 1.683$, $df = 2$, $p < 0.5$
L: $x^2 = 0.205$, $df = 2$, $p < 0.95$
EA: $x^2 = 2.959$, $df = 2$, $p < 0.3$.

Table 16. Percentage (nr in parenthesis) of SE judgments at each test for each cluster of items.

	Pretest	Training test	Posttest
CS			
Exper.	0	66.7% (10)	73.3% (11)
Contr.	12.5% (2)	68.8% (11)	81.3% (13)
L			
Exper.	6.7% (1)	80.0% (12)	66.7% (10)
Contr.	6.3% (1)	68.8% (11)	75.0% (12)
EA			
Exper.	20.0% (3)	73.3% (11)	93.3% (14)
Contr.	0	75.0% (12)	87.5% (14)

The spontaneous developmental tendencies are summarized in Table 17. In the experimental group 3 subjects (75%) moved from the lower to the higher phase during the time between Training and Posttest, while only 2 SE subjects

(18.2%) moved downwards. In the control group 75% of the OA subjects moved upwards and 8.3% moved downwards. The difference between the groups was not significant ($x^2 = 0.221$, df = 1, p < 0.7), such as the difference between the upward and downward tendencies inside the groups (Exp.: $x^2 = 1.832$, df = 1, p < 0.2; Contr.: $x^2 = 3.517$, df = 1, p < 0.1).

Table 17. Percentage (nr of Ss in parenthesis) spontaneous developmental tendencies between Training test and Posttest for Experimental and Control groups.

	OA→SE	SE→OA
Exper.	75.0% (3)	18.2% (2)
Contr.	75.0% (3)	8.3% (1)

There was not any difference in the age of the controls who moved to the SE phase after the Instruction and those who did not. On the other hand the observed difference in the experimental group at both Training and Posttest was not significant. A Mann-Whitney U test (Mendenhall, McClave & Ramey, 1977) at Training test showed that U = 21.5, p < 0.47, and at Posttest U = 5.5, p < 0.14 (Table 18).

Table 18. Mean age for SE and OA judgments (nr of Ss in parenthesis) at each test for the Experimental and Control groups.

	Pretest	Training test	Posttest
Exper.			
SE	—	6y,3m (11)	6y,3m (12)
OA	6y,3m (15)	6y,2m (4)	5y,11m (3)
Contr.			
SE	—	6y,4m (12)	6y,4m (14)
OA	6y,4m (16)	6y,4m (4)	6y,4m (2)

Discussion

The results of this study supported the first hypothesis that the Instruction promotes a quick, high, generalizable and stable shift to the higher phase of moral judgment. Although the mean age of the subjects was approximately one year lower than the age of the subjects in the previous study, 73.3% of the experimentals and 75% of the controls moved to the SE phase. At Posttest, three weeks later, it was shown that the corresponding percentage was

80% and 87.5%, which means not only stability and generality but a slight movement upwards as well. These results repeated the findings of the previous study and strengthened the conclusion that the presentation of simple instructions accelerates the development of moral judgment.

The second and main hypothesis of this study was also supported. The effect of the Instruction was not dependent on the personal authority of the experimenter (instructor—tester), since the development did not accelerate at a significantly different rate between the Experimental and Control groups. The same results were obtained for each cluster of items separately. Furthermore, no significant difference was obtained in the spontaneous developmental tendencies between the two groups, although either the upward or downward tendencies were significantly different. Thus, the hypothesis that the Instruction was the main factor which initiated the development to the higher phase now has stronger support.

The controversial age results of the previous study did not appear in the present study. That could be dependent on the lower age of the subjects in this study. Furthermore, no age difference at all was found between the controls who internalized the Instruction and those who did not. Compared to the age results of the previous study, the present age results show that children younger than the seventh year of age are much more eager to accept the Instruction than the subjects who are one year older.

Unfortunately, it was impossible to find a greater number of Greek-speaking children at an age corresponding to that of the previous study, since this population is very small in Sweden. Nevertheless, the younger age of the subjects allows us to maintain that suitable instructions can accelerate the development of moral judgment even for younger children.

CRITIQUE AND CONCLUSIONS

Methodological problems

The use of the original Piagetian story items constitutes a major methodological problem for these studies. Since Piaget constructed these stories more than fifty years ago and for his interviews with Swiss children, one may wonder if these are suitable for use today in a different society. Unfortunately, this problem can not be solved in the framework of a purely psychological study. For the construction of representative story items a special study is necessary in order to describe the moral thinking of the children in a concrete place and time. Any other solution, e.g., the construction of other new stories by the experimenter without conducting a special study does not provide any real solution to this problem. The problem of the fitness of the items would be present even with these newly constructed stories.

A similar kind of critique can be directed towards the Instruction used in the present studies. Many questions may arise about the form of that Instruction. Does it match the aims of the studies? Could one improve it by changing it in any way? In order to answer these and other questions it is necessary to conduct a special study for the construction of instructions. We could then explain why these and not others are better in promoting moral development. Unfortunately, the development of the Instruction was based solely on the theory of Vygotsky about the development of logico-mathematical thought and not on a study investigating its relation to moral thought.

Another similar problem concerns the selection of the evaluation criteria. These are also based on Piaget's theory about what characterizes and differentiates the higher from the lower phase of moral thinking. Nor were these criteria the outcome of an empirical study of the reality of today. Such a study could provide a contemporary answer to the description of the characteristics of thought at each phase and give us the possibility to compare the justifications of the instructed SE subjects with the answers of uninstructed SE subjects.

When we are studying moral thought it is very important to clarify whether the items and the method used are valid for the sample of the study, since it is assumed that the content of moral thought is much more dependent on the time and place factors than the content of thinking about physical conditions and relations, despite the fact that these studies were focused on the cognitive processes and not on the moral content. Thus, a new description of the contemporary moral principles, thoughts, ideas, such as of the social situations and relations may be regarded as necessary. The same problem may arise about the sex of the subjects. The results showed that there was not any significant difference between boys and girls, but the question of the role played by the content of the items remains. That content was social knowledge, ideologically coloured, and it is widely accepted that such knowledge discriminates between the two sexes and is different in other places and times. However, although these studies did not test the identity of physical and moral cognitive processes, the results obtained are not incompatible with such a hypothesis. In that respect the content of the items would not be significant.

The present work was limited only to the study of the development of moral judgment. The method which was used focused solely on cognitive processes. The items consisted of stories that may be of little significance for the subjects. Furthermore, there were only two concepts that were examined: the concept of intention and the concept of equality. Of course, this is not sufficient for coming to a definite conclusion about the influence of instructions on moral development. We have to study moral thinking and moral action combined. A conclusion concerned with the development of thought may not be considered as very important for theorizing inside the framework of a Piagetian theory, since the drive to adapt to reality (physical and social) is supposed to be the cause of development. In order to adapt one has not only to equilibrate his cognitive processes but also to let them guide his action in the real world. According to Piaget, the separation of thought and action in the adaptive effort of the child is impossible. Yet, one can not rely solely on the use of the Piagetian story items in order to make conclusions about the whole moral development.

Another problem, very close to the issue of thought and action, is the problem of the generality of the results to real life. Although the effect of the Instruction was stable over time and generalized to new story items, it is not certain that it is generalizable to real life situations, i.e., when the child morally judges the actions of his friends or his own actions. Neither is it confirmed that the higher moral thought attained in the laboratory is going to guide the subject's moral action there or in the world outside. Thus, all the questions about the relation of moral thought to moral action remain unanswered here.

The Instruction could have a different effect on moral development, if it were limited to the disconfirmation of the "wrong" answers given by the subjects and had not been extended to the presentation and the explanation of the "right" answers. A separation of the Instruction in these two parts could provide the opportunity to test the Piagetian disequilibration against the instruction theory of Vygotsky. It could be supposed that the disconfirmation of the "wrong" answer may cause disequilibrium, which is necessary for the onset of the developmental process, whereas the form of the instruction used in the present studies causes not only disequilibrium but gives a solution to that as well. On the other hand, the aim of these studies was not to test the theories of Piaget and Vygotsky, but to explore the influence of instruction on the development of moral thought. A test of these theories demands much more than a simple separation of the instruction, especially in the area of moral development since the original Piagetian theory (1932) did not incorporate instruction in more than a limited reference to the role of a collaborator, and Vygotsky did not develop a theory of moral thinking.

The experimental design used in these empirical studies may be accused of allowing some learning effect to play a role in the acceleration of development. That is more true for the first study, where the controls did not receive an alternative Instruction and Training test. On the other hand, if the learning effect was so strong, one would expect that the upward movement should continue at Posttest as well, but that was not shown. The results at both Training test and Posttest, in both studies, were at the same level.

It seems very strange to use the instruction of an authority, i.e., the experimenter, in order to cause independence from authority constraint. This paradox may be resolved if we proceed to a deeper analysis of the developmental processes. But we may hypothesize that some kind of higher authority is always necessary to cause disequilibrium, i.e., for the acceptance of the instruction by the child so it can be contrasted to his prevalent mode of thinking. Otherwise the child would not admit the instruction, with no disequilibrium and cognitive reorganization as a result.

Conclusion

The results of these empirical studies showed that it is possible to aid the development of children's moral thinking by giving to them suitable instructions. Of course this development consists only of a shift to subjective thinking and a liberation from authority constraint in judging the fairness of the actions of hypothetical story characters. Furthermore, this development goes towards a more abstract thinking which could be more functional thinking. That means that, if the child transformed and applied the higher form of moral thinking in a real situation, it could result in a better adaptation to that social reality. All this arises from the fact that the items and the variables used in these studies were Piagetian, i.e., the results show that it could be possible to accelerate the development towards Piagetian moral autonomy by using suitable instructions, since Piaget's theory implies some analogy between the concepts tested here and the autonomy function.

On the other hand, the previous results do not provide any definite evidence about the influence of instructions on the acceleration of moral development towards independent production of concepts, schemes, and rules. The results do not confirm any shift to autonomous moral thinking and action as Piaget meant it. The issue of autonomy can be studied only in a real situation where both thinking and action are involved.

Nevertheless, the results of the present studies give us the possibility to hypothesize that instructions may promote the development of autonomous moral thinking and action. That was not clear in the research done before. The Kohlbergian studies of the acceleration of moral development by any kind of intervention were limited to the concrete-abstract dimension of the six stage scale. The Learning approach focused only on the lower automatic processes which control moral action. And the few attempts to study the role of instruction in Piagetian terms did not investigate it as a means towards autonomy, and could not give an adequate theoretical explanation for its effect on moral development. Of course it is necessary to conduct new studies in different areas of the issue of moral development. Such studies could be: (1) a test of the impact of instructions on the development of moral thought and action, (2) the construction of instructions adapted to a social situation of a concrete place and time, and (3) the use of these instructions in an applied study in real situations as schools, homes, youth centers, etc. Although it has not been confirmed that the instruction did accelerate, or initiate the development towards autonomy, the present studies constitute a first step in this area of research.

REFERENCES

Aronfreed, J. The nature, variety, and social patterning of moral responses to transgression. *J. Abn. Soc. Psychol.*, 1961, *63*, 223—240.

Aronfreed, J. The effects of experimental socialization paradigms upon two moral responses to transgression. *J. Abn. Soc. Psychol.*, 1963, *66*, 437—448.

Aronfreed, J. The concept of internalization. In D. A. Goslin (Ed) *Handbook of socialization theory and research*. Chicago: Rand McNally, 1969.

Aronfreed, J. Moral development from the standpoint of a general psychological theory. In T. Lickona (Ed) *Moral development and behavior*. New York: Holt, Rinehart & Winston, 1976.

Aronfreed, J., Cutick, R., & Fagen, S. Cognitive structure, punishment, and nurturance in the experimental induction of self-criticism. *Child Development*, 1963, *34*, 281—294.

Aronfreed, J., & Reber, A. Internalized behavioral suppression and the timing of social punishment. *J. Pers. Soc. Psychol.*, 1965, *1*, 3—16.

Bandura, A. Social learning theory of identificatory processes. In D. A. Goslin (Ed) *Handbook of socialization theory and research*. Chicago: Rand McNally, 1969.

Bandura, A. *Social learning theory*. Englewood Cliffs, N.J.: Prentice Hall, 1977.

Bandura, A., & McDonald, F. Influence of social reinforcement and the behavior of models in shaping children's moral judgments. *J. Abn. Soc. Psychol.*, 1963, *67*, 274—281.

Baumrind, D. A dialectical materialist's perspective on knowing social reality. *New Directions for Child Development*, 1978, *2*, 61—82.

Bergling, K. *Moral development: The validity of Kohlberg's theory*. Stockholm: Almqvist & Wiksell, 1981.

Bergling, K. *Moralutveckling*. Stockholm: LiberFörlag, 1982.

Blasi, A. Bridging moral cognition and moral action: A critical review of the literature. *Psychological Bulletin*, 1980, *88*, 1—45.

Blasi, A. Moral cognition and moral action: A theoretical perspective. *Developmental Review*, 1983, *3*, 178—210.

Brainerd, C.J. *Piaget's theory of intelligence*. Englewood Cliffs, N.J.: Prentice Hall, 1978.

Broughton, J. The cognitive-developmental approach to morality: A reply to Kurtines & Greif. *J. Moral Education*, 1978, *7*, 81—96.

Chomsky, N. On cognitive structures and their development: A reply to Piaget. In M. Piattelli-Palmarini (Ed) *Language and learning*. London: RKP, 1980.

Colby, A., Kohlberg, L., Gibbs, J., & Lieberman, M. A longitudinal study of moral judgment. *Monographs of the Society for Research in Child Development*, 1983, *48*, (1, Serial No. 200).

Cowan, P.A., Langer, J., Heavenrich, J., & Nathanson, M. Social learning and Piaget's cognitive theory of moral development. *J. Pers. Soc. Psychol.*, 1969, 11, 261—274.

Crowley, P.M. Effect of training upon objectivity of moral judgment in grade-school children. *J. Pers. Soc. Psychol.*, 1968, *8*, 228—232.

Damon, W. Early conceptions of positive justice as related to the development of logical operations. *Child Development*, 1975, *46*, 301—312.

Damon, W. *The social world of the child*. San Francisco: Jossey-Bass, 1977.

Damon, W. Patterns of change in children's social reasoning: A two year longitudinal study. *Child Development*, 1980, *51*, 1010—1017.

Damon, W. Self-understanding and moral development from childhood to adolescence. In W. Kurtines & J. Gewirtz (Eds) *Morality, moral behavior and moral development*. New York: Wiley, 1984.

Damon, W., & Hart, D. The development of self-understanding from infancy through adolescence. *Child Development*, 1982, *53*, 841—864.

Damon, W., & Killen, M. Peer interaction and the process of change in children's moral reasoning. *Merrill-Palmer Quarterly*, 1982, *28*, 347—367.

Emler, N. Morality and politics: The ideological dimensions in the theory of moral development. In H. Weinreich-Haste & D. Locke (Eds) *Morality in the making*. New York: Wiley, 1983a.

Emler, N. Approaches to moral development: Piagetian influences. In S. Mogdil, C. Mogdil, & G. Brown (Eds) *Jean Piaget: An interdisciplinary critique*. London: RKP, 1983b.

Freud, S. *Orientering i psykoanalys*. Stockholm: Natur och Kultur, 1940/1976.

Gibbs, J. Kohlberg's stages of moral judgment: A constructive critique. *Harvard Educational Review*, 1977, *47*, 43—61.

Gibbs, J. Kohlberg's moral stage theory: A Piagetian revision. *Human Development*, 1979, *22*, 89—112.

Gibbs,J., Arnild, K., & Burkhart, J. Sex differences in the expression of moral judgment. *Child Development*, 1984, *55*, 1040—1043.

Gibbs, J., Clark, P., Joseph, J., Green, J., Goodrick, T., & Makowski, D. Relations between moral judgment, moral courage, and field independence. *Child Development*, 1986, *57*, 185—193.

Gillingan, C. In a different voice: Women's conceptions of self and of morality. *Harvard Educational Review*, 1977, *47*, 481—517.

Guilford, J.P. *Foundamental statistics in psychology and education*. New York: McGraw-Hill, 1956.

Haan, N., Smith, B., & Block, J. Moral reasoning of young adults: Political-social behavior, family background, and personality correlates. *J. Pers. Soc. Psychol.*, 1968, *10*, 183—201.

Haan, N., Weiss, R., & Johnson, V. The role of logic in moral reasoning and development. *Developmental Psychology*, 1982, *18*, 245—256.

Higgins, A., Power, C., & Kohlberg, L. The relationship of moral atmosphere to judgments of responsibility. In W. Kurtines & J. Gewirtz (Eds) *Morality, moral behavior, and moral development*. New York: Wiley, 1984.

Karpova, S.N., & Petrushina, L.G. Significance of games involving a plot and a role-playing for the development of moral behavior. *Soviet Psychology*, 1982/1983, *21*, 18—31.

Kohlberg, L. The development of children's orientations toward a moral order. *Vita Humana*, 1963, *6*, 11—33.

Kohlberg, L. Moral education in the schools: A developmental view. *The School Review*, 1966, *74*, 1—30.

Kohlberg, L. Stage and sequence: The cognitive-developmental approach to socialization. In D.A. Goslin (Ed) *Handbook of socialization theory and research*. Chicago: Rand McNally, 1969.

Kohlberg, L. Moral stages and moralization: The cognitive developmental approach. In T. Lickona (Ed) *Moral development and behavior*. New York: Holt, Rinehart & Winston, 1976.

Kohlberg, L. *The philosophy of moral development*. San Francisco: Harper & Row, 1981.

Kohlberg, L. *The psychology of moral development*. San Francisco: Harper & Row, 1984.

Kohlberg, L. The just community: Approach to moral education in theory an practice. In M. Berkowitz & F. Oser (Eds) *Moral education: Theory and application*. Hillsdale, N.J.: LEA, 1985.

Kohlberg, L., & Candee, D. The relationship of moral judgment to moral action. In L. Kohlberg *The psychology of moral development*. San Francisco: Harper & Row, 1984a.

Kohlberg, L., & Candee, D. The relationship of moral judgment to moral action. In W. Kurtines & J. Gewirtz (Eds) *Morality, moral behavior, and moral development*. New York: Wiley, 1984b.

Kohlberg, L., & Kramer, R. Continuities and discontinuities in childhood and adult moral development. *Human Development*, 1969, *12*, 93—120.

Kohlberg, L., Higgins, A., Tappan, M., & Schrader, D. From substages to moral types: Heteronomous and autonomous morality. In L. Kohlberg *The psychology of moral development*. San Francisco: Harper & Row, 1984.

Krebs, D., & Gillmore, J. The relationship among the first stages of cognitive development, role-taking abilities, and moral development. *Child Development*, 1982, *53*, 877—886.

Kugiumutzakis, J. The origin, development, and function of the early infant imitation. Unpublished doctoral dissertation, Uppsala University, 1985.

Kurtines, W., & Greif, E. The development of moral thought: Review and evaluation of Kohlberg's approach. *Psychological Bulletin*, 1974, *81*, 453—470.

Lickona, T. The acceleration of children's judgments about responsibility: An experimental test of Piaget's hypotheses about the causes of moral judgmental change. Unpublished doctoral dissertation, State University of New York at Albany, 1971.

Lickona, T. Research on Piaget's theory of moral development. In T. Lickona (Ed) *Moral development and behavior*. New York: Holt, Rinehart & Winston, 1976.

Loevinger, J. The meaning and measurement of ego development. *American Psychologist*, 1966, *21*, 195—206.

Loevinger, J. *Ego development*. San Francisco: Jossey-Bass, 1976.

Mendenhall, W., McClave, J.T., & Ramey, M. *Statistics for psychology*. North Scituate, Mass.: Duxbury, 1977.

Milgram, S. Behavioral study of obedience. *J. Abn. Soc. Psychol.*, 1963, *67*, 371—378.

Moir, D.J. Egocentrism and the emergence of conventional morality in preadolescent girls. *Child Development*, 1974, *45*, 299—304.

Nisan, M., & Kohlberg, L. Universality and variation in moral judgment: A longitudinal and cross-sectional study in Turkey. *Child Development*, 1982, *53*, 865—876.

Nucci, L. Conceptions of personal issues: A domain distinct from moral or societal concepts. *Child Development*, 1981, *52*, 114—121.

Nucci, L., & Nucci, M. Children's responses to moral and social conventional transgressions in free-play settings. *Child Development*, 1982a, *53*, 1337—1342.

Nucci, L., & Nucci, M. Children's social interactions in the context of moral and conventional transgressions. *Child Development*, 1982b, *53*, 403—412.

Nucci, L., & Turiel, E. Social interactions and the development of social concepts in preschool children. *Child Development*, 1978, *49*, 400—407.

Page, R. Longitudinal evidence for the sequentiality of Kohlberg's stages of moral judgment in adolescent males. *J. Genetic Psychol.*, 1981, *139*, 3—9.

Parikh, B. Development of moral judgment and its relation to family environmental factors in Indian and American families. *Child Development*, 1980, *51*, 1030—1039.

Piaget, J. *The moral judgment of the child*. London: RKP, 1932.

Piaget, J. *The origin of intelligence in the child*. Harmondsworth, Middlesex: Penguin, 1936.

Piaget, J. *Comments on Vygotsky's critical remarks*. Cambridge, Mass.: The MIT Press, 1962.

Piaget, J. *Frumtidens skola*. Lund: Forum, 1972.

Piaget, J. *The grasp of consciousness*. London: RKP, 1976.

Piaget, J. *Success and understanding*. London: RKP, 1978.

Piaget, J. *Experiments in contradiction*. Chicago: Chicago University Press, 1980.

Piaget, J., & Inhelder, B. *The psychology of the child*. London: RKP, 1969.

Rest, J. The hierarchical nature of moral judgment: A study of patterns of comprehension and preference of moral stages. *J. Pers.*, 1973, *41*, 86—108.

Rest, J. *Revised manual for the Defining Issues Test*. Minneapolis: Minnesota Moral Research Projects, 1979.

Rest, J., Turiel, E., & Kohlberg, L. Level of moral development as a determinant of preference and comprehension of moral judgments made by others. *J. Pers.*, 1969, *37*, 225—252.

Snarey, J.R. Cross-cultural universality of social-moral development: A critical review of Kohlbergian research. *Psychological Bulletin*, 1985, *97*, 202—232.

Subbotskii, E.V. Development of moral behavior in preschoolers in a psychological-pedagogical experiment. *Soviet Psychology*, 1981, *20*, 62—80.

Subbotskii, E.V. Shaping moral actions in children. *Soviet Psychology*, 1983a, *22*(1), 56—71.

Subbotskii, E.V. The moral development of the preschool child. *Soviet Psychology*, 1983b, *22*(3), 3—19.

Tapp, J.L., & Kohlberg, L. Developing senses of law and legal justice. *J. Social Issues*, 1971, *27*, 65—91.

Tomlinson-Keasy, C., & Keasy, C.B. The mediating role of cognitive development in moral judgment. *Child Development*, 1974, *45*, 291—298.

Tudge, J. Moral development in the Soviet Union: A conceptual framework. *Soviet Psychology*, 1983, *22*, 3—12.

Turiel, E. An experimental test of the sequentiality of developmental stages in the child's moral judgments. *J. Pers. Soc. Psychol.*, 1966, *3*, 611—618.

Turiel, E. Developmental processes in the child's moral thinking. In P. Mussen et al. (Eds) *Trends and issues in developmental psychology*. New York: Halt, Rinehart & Winston, 1969.

Turiel, E. Conflict and transition in adolescent moral development. *Child Development*, 1974, *45*, 14—29.

Turiel, E. Conflict and transition in adolescent moral development, II: The resolution of disequilibrium through structural reorganization. *Child Development*, 1977, *48*, 634—637.

Turiel, E. *The development of social knowledge: Morality and convention*. Cambridge: Cambridge University Press, 1983.

Turiel, E., & Rothman, G.R. The influence of reasoning on behavioral choices at different stages on moral development. *Child Development*, 1972, *43*, 741—756.

Vine, I. The nature of moral commitments. In H. Weinreich-Haste & D. Locke (Eds) *Morality in the making*. New York: Wiley, 1983.

Vygotsky, L.S. *Thought and language*. Cambridge, Mass.: The MIT Press, 1962.

Vygotsky, L.S. *Mind in society*. Cambridge, Mass.: Harvard University Press, 1978.

Walker, L. The sequentiality of Kohlberg's stages of moral development. *Child Development*, 1982, *53*, 1330—1336.

Weinreich-Haste, H. Kohlberg's theory of moral development. In H. Weinreich-Haste & D. Locke (Eds) *Morality in the making*. New York: Wiley, 1983.

Yakobson, S.G., & Pocherevina, L.P. The role of subjective attitude toward ethical models in the regulation of preschooler's moral conduct. *Soviet Psychology*, 1983, *22*, 20—37.

Yannopoulos-Mitsacos, J. Relationships of parental attitudes to moral development of a selected group of greek children, age 5,0—6,0. Unpublished doctoral dissertation, Ball State University, Muncie, Indiana, 1984.

APPENDIX A
THE PIAGETIAN MORAL STORIES

(Translated to Greek. Yannopoulos-Mitsacos, 1984)

Stories of Clumsiness and Stealing (CS)

CS I

(A) A little boy named Giannis is in his room. He is called to dinner. He goes into the dining room. But behind the door there is a chair, and on the chair there is a tray with fifteen cups on it. Giannis couldn't have known that all this was behind the door. He goes in, the door knocks against the tray, bang go the fifteen cups and they all get broken.

(B) Once there was a little boy whose name was Aris. One day when his mother was out he tried to get some jam out of the cupboard. He climbed up onto a chair but he couldn't reach it. However, while he was trying to get it he knocked over a cup. The cup fell down and broke.

CS II

(A) Katerina had a little friend who kept a bird in a cage. Katerina thought the bird was very unhappy, and she was always asking her friend to let him out, but the friend wouldn't. So one day when her friend wasn't there, Katerina stole the bird. She let it fly away and hid the cage in the attic so that the bird would never be shut up in it again.

(B) Joulia stole some candy from her mother one day when her mother was not there. She hid and ate them.

CS III

(A) Antonis meets a friend who is very poor. This friend tells him that he has had no dinner that day because there was nothing to eat at his home. Then Antonis goes into a baker's shop, and since he has no money, he waits until the baker's back is turned and steals a roll. Then he runs out and gives the roll to his friend.

(B) Margarita goes into a shop. She sees a pretty piece of ribbon on a table and thinks to herself that it would look very nice on her dress. So, while the saleslady's back is turned, she steals the ribbon and runs away at once.

Stories of Lying (L)

L I

(A) A little boy goes for a walk in the street and meets a big dog who frightens him very much. He goes home and tells his mother he has seen a dog that was big as a cow.

(B) A child comes home from school and tells his mother that the teacher has given him good marks, but it is not true; the teacher has given him no marks at all, either good or bad. His mother is very pleased and rewards him.

L II

(A) A boy was playing in his room. His mother called and asked him to deliver a message for her. He didn't feel like going out, so he told his mother that his feet were hurting. But it wasn't true. His feet weren't hurting him in the least.

(B) A boy wanted very much to go for a ride in a car, but no one ever asked him. One day he saw a man driving a beautiful car. When he got home he told his parents that the gentleman in the car had stopped and had taken him for a little drive. But it wasn't true; he had made it all up.

L III

(A) A boy couldn't draw very well, but he would have liked very much to be able to draw. One day he was looking at a beautiful drawing that another boy had done, and he said: "I made that drawing."

(B) A boy was playing with the scissors one day when his mother was out and he lost them. When his mother came in he said that he hadn't seen them and hadn't touched them.

Stories of Equality and Authority (EA)

EA I

One Thursday afternoon, a mother asked her little girl and boy to help her around the house because she was tired. The girl was to dry the plates and the boy was to fetch some wood. But the little boy went out and played in the street, so the mother asked the other one to do all the work. What did she say?

EA II

Once there was a family with three brothers. The two younger brothers were twins. They all used to polish their shoes every morning. One day the oldest brother was ill, so the mother asked one of the others to polish the brother's shoes as well as his own. What do you think of that?

EA III

A father had two boys. One of them always grumbled when he was sent on messages. The other one didn't like being sent either, but he always went without saying a word. So the father used to send the boy who didn't grumble more often than the other one. What do you think of that?

APPENDIX B
INTERVIEW QUESTIONS

(Yannopoulos-Mitsacos, 1984)

Questions for Clumsiness and Stealing (CS) stories

All stories
*Did you understand these two stories?
*What did the first child do?
*What did the second child do?

CS I

*Is one child naughtier than the other? Why? (Regardless of the child's answer that one child is naughtier than the other, or that both children are naughty, ask again "why?" and repeat the question asking which child is the naughtier).
*If you were this child's (these children's) mommy (or daddy) would you punish both children the same? (If the answer is "no", then ask, "whom would you punish more?" If the answer is "because he is naughtier", ask again "why?"

CS II & CS III

*Is one child naughtier than the other? Why? (Ask "why" regardless of a positive or a negative answer to the first question).
*Why did Katerina/Antonis steal the bird/roll?
*Why did Joulia/Margarita steal the candy/ribbon? (For both these questions ask for more details — indirectly if you consider the answer inadequate).
*Whom would you punish more?
(And depending on the answer)
*Why would you punish them both? or
*Why would you punish Katerina/Antonis more? or
*Why would you punish Joulia/Margarita more?
(And then)
*Is Katerina/Antonis naughtier than Joulia/Margarita? (Or vice versa).
*Why?

Questions for Lying (L) stories

*Tell me what happened in the stories I just told you?
*Which one is the naughtiest child?
*Why?
(If the child makes it a point that in the one story mommy knows that this is an obvious lie, then ask *again*):
*What makes one lie different from the other?
(From the child's answer, try to detect if deceiving the adult in an "incredible-exaggerated" manner is a worse lie. Does the child justify the lie because of the story character's emotions? Does this make the one character naughtier than the other or the other way round?)
*If you were the mommy (or daddy) and knew that both of these children were lying, whom would you punish the most?

Questions for Equality and Authority (EA) stories

*Tell me the whole story now.

*Was it okay that the little girl/boy did her/his brother's job as well? (If the child answers "no" ask "why"; if the child answers "yes" then proceed to the following question).

*Why? Was this fair (just, correct) or she/he had to do it because mommy/daddy asked her/him to?

(And depending on the child's answer)

*Why was it fair? or

*Why was it unfair?

(With this last question we want to make sure how consistent the child's answer is).

APPENDIX C
THE PICTURES OF THE STORIES

(Yannopoulos-Mitsacos, 1984)

1. CS I
2. CS II
3. CS III
4. L I
5. L II A
6. L II B
7. L III A
8. L III B
9. EA I
10. EA II
11. EA III

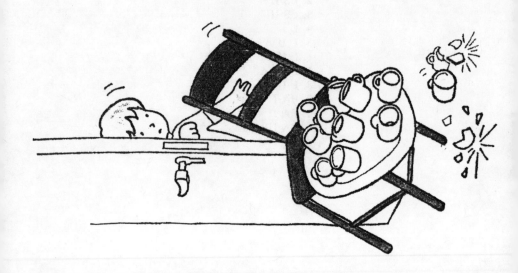

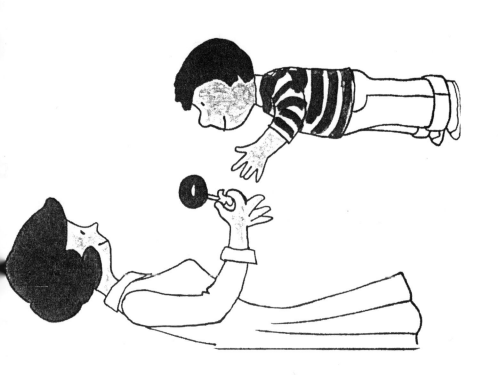

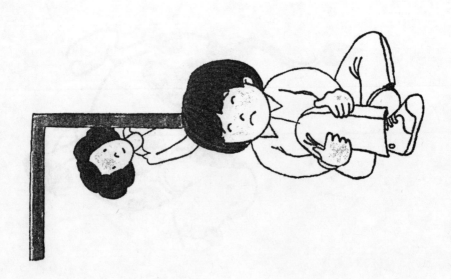

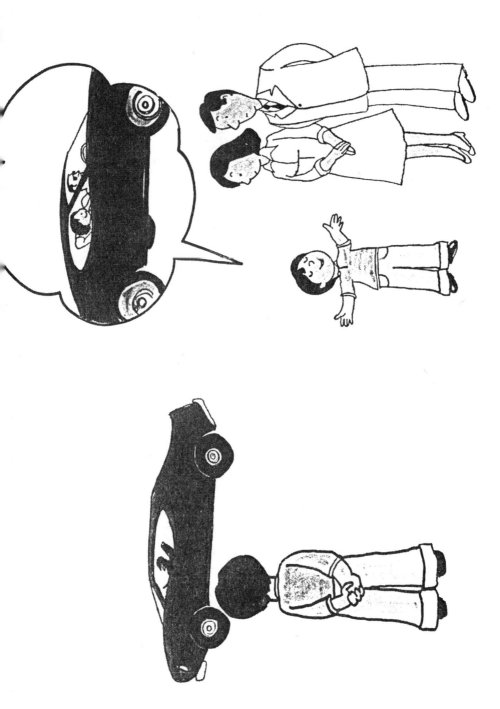

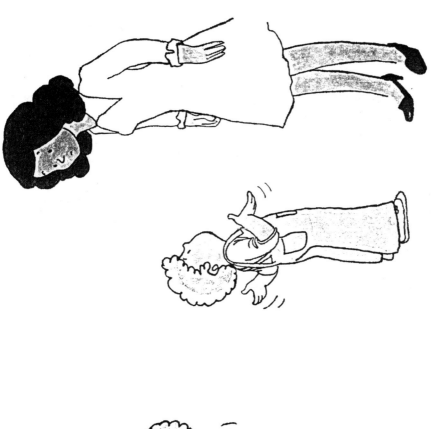

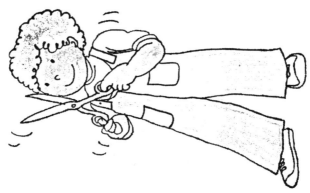

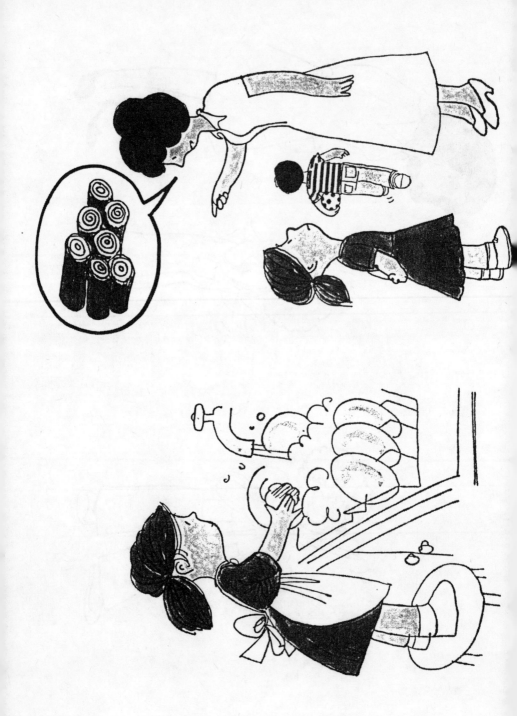

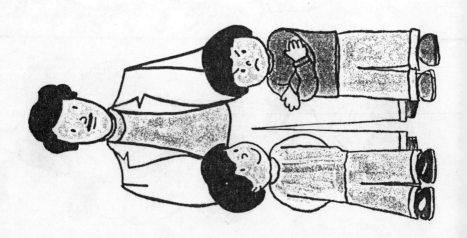